Gregory J. Manin Alicia Artusi Robert Quinn

# engage

2nd edition

Student Book

| Reading | Listening | Speaking | Writing |
| --- | --- | --- | --- |
| | | | |
| Friend finder profiles<br>Acting school<br>Reading skills: Getting a general idea | New friends | Talking about likes and dislikes<br>Pronunciation: Sentence stress | A personal profile<br>Writing skills: Paragraphs |
| South American Express!<br>Pet Airways | At the transportation museum<br>Listening skills: Listening for key words | Talking about rules<br>Pronunciation: Weak vowels (*can / can't*) | An e-mail about a trip |
| | | | |
| Witness statements<br>Dumb criminals<br>Reading skills: Using pictures and titles | Describing what you were doing | Expressing surprise<br>Pronunciation: /uː/ and /ʊ/ sounds | Telling a story<br>Writing skills: Avoiding repetition |
| *2012*: The movie<br>A Story of Survival<br>Reading skills: Summarizing a text | Apologizing<br>Listening skills: Previewing the questions | Giving excuses<br>Pronunciation: /iː/ and /ɪ/ sounds | A movie summary<br>Writing skills: Narrative linkers |
| | | | |
| Best friends, different styles<br>Serious Styling | Comparing clothes<br>Listening skills: Discussing your ideas | At a clothes store<br>Pronunciation: Linked sounds | My favorite person<br>Writing skills: Order of adjectives |
| That's a record!<br>Youth travel<br>Reading skills: Scanning quickly for information | At the travel agency | Giving advice<br>Pronunciation: /s/ and /ʃ/ sounds | A vacation brochure<br>Writing skills: Checking your grammar and spelling |
| | | | |
| Summer Sports Resolutions<br>Hit the snow | Talking about vacation plans<br>Listening skills: Predicting main ideas | Talking about plans<br>Pronunciation: /g/ and /ŋ/ sounds | Summer sports plans<br>Writing skills: *also* and *too* |
| Friend finder chat<br>School news | Talking about arrangements | Making arrangements<br>Pronunciation: *would you* elision | An invitation<br>Writing skills: *so* |

# Welcome

## Vocabulary

### Weather

**1** Fill in the blanks with the words below. Then listen, check, and repeat.

cloudy cold hot ~~raining~~ snowing stormy sunny windy

1 It's *raining* ............ in Bangkok.

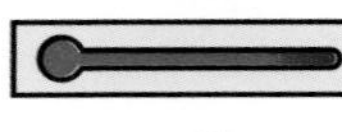
2 It's ............ in Chicago.

3 It's ............ in Lima.

4 It's ............ in Moscow.

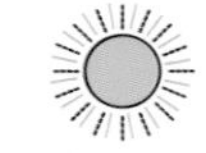
5 It's ............ in Mumbai.

6 It's ............ in Sydney.

7 It's ............ in Tokyo.

8 It's ............ in Zurich.

**2** **Over to you!**

What's the weather like today?

### Clothes

**3** Unscramble the letters. Then listen, check, and repeat.

1 rhsit *shirt*
2 spnat ............
3 csosk ............
4 ehsso ............
5 seslgas ............
6 otp ............
7 ksitr ............
8 tobos ............

### Physical descriptions

**4** Fill in the blanks with the words below. Then listen, check, and repeat.

beard ~~blond~~ dark eyes hair mustache straight wavy

Lydia has light (1) *blond* ............ hair and blue (2) ............ . Her (3) ............ isn't wavy – it's long and very (4) ............ .

Marcos has brown eyes and (5) ............ brown hair – it's short and (6) ............ . He has a (7) ............ , but he doesn't have a (8) ............ .

**5** **Over to you!**

Write sentences to describe a friend. Write about their physical appearance and the clothes they are wearing today.

### Possessions

**6** Match the pictures with the words below. Then listen, check, and repeat.

backpack belt bracelet earrings key key ring ~~ID card~~

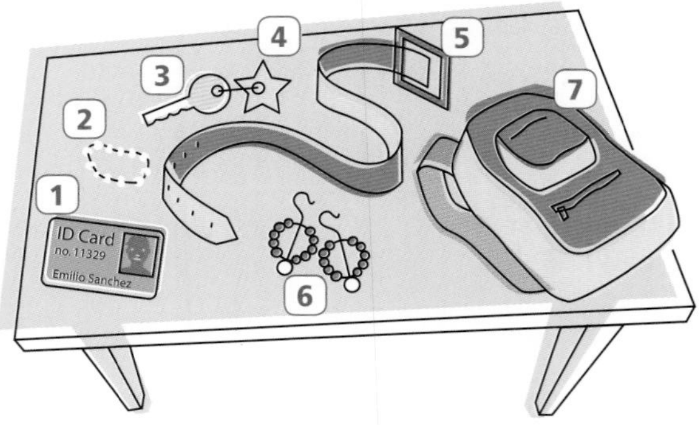


1 *ID card*
2 ............
3 ............
4 ............
5 ............
6 ............
7 ............



Workbook p.W2

## Food and drink

**1** **Fill in the blanks with the words below. Then listen, check, and repeat.**

apple coffee ~~eggs~~ French fries hamburger milk pizza salad sausages soda

For breakfast, Miranda is having two (1) *eggs* ______ with some (2) ______. She's drinking (3) ______.

For lunch, she's having a (4) ______ with cheese, and some (5) ______. She's drinking (6) ______.

For dinner, Miranda's having some (7) ______ with a green (8) ______, and she's drinking (9) ______. For dessert, she's having an (10) ______.

**2** **Over to you!**

**What do you usually have for breakfast, lunch, and dinner? Make three lists and compare with a friend.**

## Jobs

**3** **Fill in the blanks with the words below. Then listen, check, and repeat.**

architect artist fashion designer inventor ~~musician~~ politician scientist writer

1 Elvis Presley was a rock *musician* ______.
2 William Lamb was an ______. He designed the Empire State Building.
3 Agatha Christie was a famous ______. She wrote mystery novels.
4 John Logie Baird was the ______ of the TV.
5 Marie Curie was a ______. She studied physics and chemistry.
6 Gianni Versace was a ______. He created beautiful clothes.
7 Georgia O'Keeffe was an ______. She painted many pictures.
8 John F. Kennedy was a ______. He was president of the U.S.

## Music and musical instruments

**4** **Unscramble the letters. Then listen, check, and repeat.**

| | | | |
|---|---|---|---|
| 1 opp | *pop* | 5 sllccasia | ______ |
| 2 losu | ______ | 6 zajz | ______ |
| 3 geerga | ______ | 7 noyctru | ______ |
| 4 krco | ______ | 8 par | ______ |

**5** **Listen and write the name of the instrument.**

~~bass~~ drums guitar keyboard piano saxophone trumpet violin

| | |
|---|---|
| 1 *bass* | 5 ______ |
| 2 ______ | 6 ______ |
| 3 ______ | 7 ______ |
| 4 ______ | 8 ______ |

**6** **Over to you!**

**Write sentences about the musical instruments you and other people play.**

## Nature

**7** **Match the places. Then listen and check.**

| | |
|---|---|
| 1 Kilimanjaro | a a beach |
| 2 The Amazon | b a desert |
| 3 Madagascar | c a mountain |
| 4 Copacabana | d an island |
| 5 Mount Fuji | e a river |
| 6 The Sahara | f a volcano |

Workbook p.W3

# Grammar

## Present progressive (affirmative and negative)

**1 Look at the chart. Fill in the blanks.**

| Affirmative | Negative |
|---|---|
| I'm working now. | I (1) *'m not* working now. |
| You (2) ______ working at the moment. | You aren't working at the moment. |
| He's / She's / It's working today. | He / She / It (3) ______ working today. |
| We (4) ______ / You're / They're working now. | We / You / They (5) ______ working now. |

**2 Circle the correct words.**

1 We's / (We're) reading at the moment.
2 He isn't / He aren't getting dressed now.
3 I'm not / I aren't having dinner right now.
4 Shes / She's posting a comment on the Internet.
5 You're / You's doing an English exercise.
6 They aren't / They isn't wearing jeans.

**3 Complete the sentences with the verbs in parentheses. Use the present progressive.**

1 She *'s babysitting* (babysit) her brother.
2 I ______ (not watch) TV now.
3 They ______ (send) text messages.
4 He ______ (not wait) for the bus.
5 You ______ (not sleep) now.
6 I ______ (do) my homework.
7 You ______ (sit) in class now.
8 We ______ (not chat) online.

## Present progressive (questions)

**4 Look at the chart. Fill in the blanks.**

| Questions | Short answers |
|---|---|
| (1) *Am* I sitting right now? | Yes, I am. / No, I'm not. |
| (2) ______ you reading now? | Yes, you are. / No, you aren't. |
| (3) ______ he / she / it working today? | Yes, he / she / it is. No, he / she / it isn't. |
| (4) ______ we / you / they eating now? | Yes, we / you / they are. No, we / you / they aren't. |
| ***Wh-* questions** | |
| Where (5) *am* I sitting now? | |
| What (6) ______ he / she / it doing? | |
| Why (7) ______ we / you / they laughing? | |

**5 Put the words in order to make questions. Then write the answers. Use the present progressive.**

1 I / wear a baseball cap? (✗)
*Am I wearing a baseball cap*?
*No, I'm not*.

2 they / watch TV now? (✓)
______?
______.

3 she / have lunch at home? (✗)
______?
______.

4 we / do a math test today? (✓)
______?
______.

5 you / study French this year? (✗)
______?
______.

**6 Look at the underlined words in the answers. Fill in the blanks. Use the present progressive.**

1 *What* *are* you *wearing* right now?
I'm wearing <u>pants and a T-shirt</u>.
2 ______ ______ the boys ______?
They're going <u>to the museum</u>.
3 ______ ______ Mike ______?
He's running <u>because he's late</u>.
4 ______ ______ Laura ______?
She's eating <u>an apple</u>.
5 ______ ______ Jack ______?
He's studying <u>at the library</u>.

 Workbook p.W4

## Present progressive and simple present

**Take note!**

- **We use the present progressive to talk about things that are happening right now.**
  I'm wearing jeans today.
- **We use the simple present to talk about regular activities and habits. We can also use adverbs of frequency with the simple present.**
  I often wear jeans to school.

**1 Circle the correct form of the verb.**

1 I never listen / am listening to rock music.
2 Kimiko eats / is eating lunch at the moment.
3 They do / are doing their homework now.
4 It usually rains / is raining in the spring.
5 They have / are having a party today.
6 You often wear / are wearing jeans.

**2 Over to you!**

**Write sentences about three activities you do regularly and one activity you are doing now.**

## *a / an / some / any* (countable nouns)

**3 Complete the sentences with *a*, *an*, *some*, or *any*.**

1 There's a ............ sandwich on the table.
2 There aren't ............ sausages.
3 Are there ............ French fries?
4 Is there ............ egg on the table?
5 There isn't ............ banana.
6 There are ............ green apples.

## Uncountable nouns

**4 Complete the chart with the words below.**

~~backpack~~ ~~baggage~~ banana bread car chair furniture hamburger music pasta sandwich song traffic water

| Countable nouns | Uncountable nouns |
|---|---|
| backpack | baggage |
| ............ | ............ |
| ............ | ............ |
| ............ | ............ |
| ............ | ............ |
| ............ | ............ |
| ............ | ............ |

## *How much / many* + quantifiers

**5 Fill in the blanks with the words below.**

a few a lot any ~~many~~ much none

| Countable | Uncountable |
|---|---|
| How (1) many apples are there? | How much juice is there? |
| There are a lot of apples. | There's (2) ............ of juice. |
| There are (3) ............ apples. | There's a little juice. |
| There aren't many apples. | There isn't (4) ............ juice. |
| There aren't (5) ............ apples. | There isn't any juice. |
| There are none. | There's (6) ............ . |

**6 Circle the correct words.**

1 There's a lot / many of pasta, but there aren't none / any sausages.
2 How many / much salad is there? There's a few / none.
3 There isn't any / many milk, but there's a little / any soda.
4 There aren't many / much eggs, and there isn't a little / much cheese.
5 How much / many strawberries are there? There are much / a few strawberries.

→ Workbook pp.W4–W5 

# Welcome

## Possessive adjectives and pronouns

**1** **Look at the chart. Fill in the blanks.**

| Possessive adjectives | Possessive pronouns |
|---|---|
| It's my book. | It's (1) mine ........ . |
| It's (2) ................ book. | It's yours. |
| It's her book. | It's (3) ................ . |
| It's (4) ................ book. | It's his. |
| It's our book. | It's (5) ................ . |
| It's your book. | It's (6) ................ . |
| It's their book. | It's (7) ................ . |

**2** **Fill in the blanks with possessive adjectives and possessive pronouns.**

1 It's your chair. It's yours ........ .
2 They're hers. They're ................ shoes.
3 It's my skateboard. It's ................ .
4 They're ................ . They're our books.
5 It's ................ car. It's theirs.
6 They're ................ . They're his DVDs.

## *can / can't* (permission)

**Take note!**

- We use *can / can't* to ask for permission.
  Can I go out tonight? Yes, you can.
  Can I drive the car? No, you can't.

**3** **Match the sentences with the requests.**

1 There's a concert on Saturday. c
2 We saw a cat at the pet store today. ........
3 Our friends wear make-up to school. ........
4 I don't have any money for lunch. ........
5 Wow! I love your new car! ........
6 Mom! I hate the color of my hair. ........

a Can I borrow five dollars?
b Can we go for a ride later, please?
c Can we go with our friends?
d Can we buy it, please?
e Can I dye it, please?
f Can we wear it, too?

## Suggestions

**4** **Look at the pictures. Then complete the dialogues with the words below.**

about don't go great idea ~~Let's~~
not OK think way what why

1 A: Let's ........ go to the library.
B: ................ . I want to return some books.

2 A: What ................ going to the amusement park?
B: Let's ................ . It's raining right now.

3 A: ................ don't we go to the swimming pool?
B: ................ ! We can practice diving!

4 A: Why ................ we go to the coffee shop?
B: No ................ ! We always go there.

5 A: Let's ................ to the museum.
B: I don't ................ so. It's boring.

6 A: ................ about going to the skating rink?
B: That's a good ................ ! I love skating!


Workbook p.W5

## was / were

**1 Look at the chart. Fill in the blanks.**

| Affirmative | Negative |
|---|---|
| I was at home. | I (1) wasn't ........ at home. |
| You (2) ........ bored. | You weren't bored. |
| He / She / It was nice. | He / She / It (3) ........ nice. |
| We / You / They (4) ........ students. | We / You / They weren't students. |
| **Questions** | **Short answers** |
| (5) ........ I at home? | Yes, I was.<br>No, I wasn't. |
| Were you bored? | Yes, you (6) ........ .<br>No, you weren't. |
| (7) ........ he / she / it nice? | Yes, he / she / it was.<br>No, he / she / it wasn't. |
| Were we / you / they students? | Yes, we / you / they were.<br>No, we / you / they (8) ........ . |

**2 Circle the correct word.**

1 You was / (were) in my math class last year.
2 The boys **wasn't** / **weren't** very happy.
3 My sister **wasn't** / **weren't** at the skating rink.
4 We **was** / **were** hungry after the movie.
5 I **was** / **were** with Ted at the amusement park.
6 That pizza **wasn't** / **weren't** very good.

**3 Look at the names and places. Where were the people yesterday? Fill in the blanks.**

1 Was ........ Tom at the park?
Yes ........ , he was ........ .
2 ........ Liu and Sam at the library?
........ , they ........ .
3 ........ Alana at the swimming pool?
........ , she ........ .
4 ........ Eli and Ron at the shopping mall?
........ , they ........ .
5 ........ Alex at the museum?
........ , he ........ .
6 ........ Jen at the coffee shop?
........ , she ........ .

**4 Over to you!**

**Ask and answer questions about where you and your friends were last weekend.**

## Ordinal numbers

**5 Fill in the blanks with both forms of the ordinal numbers.**

| | | | |
|---|---|---|---|
| 1 | three | third | 3rd |
| 2 | nine | ........ | ........ |
| 3 | two | ........ | ........ |
| 4 | eleven | ........ | ........ |
| 5 | one | ........ | ........ |
| 6 | fourteen | ........ | ........ |
| 7 | five | ........ | ........ |
| 8 | twenty | ........ | ........ |
| 9 | sixteen | ........ | ........ |
| 10 | six | ........ | ........ |

**6 Circle the correct word.**

1 They're going to buy (four) / **fourth** tickets.
2 I was the **one** / **first** person in line.
3 It's Marc's **fifteen** / **fifteenth** birthday next Friday.
4 There are **ten** / **tenth** girls on the team.
5 The **hundred** / **hundredth** person in the store is going to win a prize.
6 She was born on May **eight** / **eighth**.
7 We saw the movie **seven** / **seventh** times.
8 Mei was the **twenty** / **twentieth** runner.

Workbook p.W5

# Welcome

## Simple past: affirmative (regular)

**1 Complete the chart with the simple past affirmative forms of the verbs below.**

~~arrive~~ change chat ~~copy~~ ~~crash~~ create die finish listen plan start ~~stop~~ study try wait watch

| Add *-d* | Add *-ed* | Change *y* to *i* and add *-ed* | Double the consonant and add *-ed* |
|---|---|---|---|
| arrived | crashed | copied | stopped |
| ........ | ........ | ........ | ........ |
| ........ | ........ | ........ | ........ |
| ........ | ........ | | |
| | ........ | | |
| | ........ | | |

## Simple past: affirmative (irregular)

**2 Fill in the blanks with the correct form of the irregular verbs.**

| Verb | Simple past |
|---|---|
| see | (1) saw |
| (2) ........ | sank |
| break | (3) ........ |
| (4) ........ | taught |
| give | (5) ........ |
| (6) ........ | took |
| win | (7) ........ |
| (8) ........ | sang |
| hit | (9) ........ |
| (10) ........ | bought |
| go | (11) ........ |
| (12) ........ | had |
| run | (13) ........ |
| (14) ........ | spent |
| tell | (15) ........ |

**Take note!**

- **In the simple past, each verb has only one affirmative form.**
- **We use the same form for all singular and plural subjects.**
  I / you / he / she / it / we / they arrived late.
  I / you / he / she / it / we / they went home.

## Simple past: negative and questions

**Take note!**

- **In the simple past negative, we put *didn't* between the subject and the base form of the verb.**
  I / you / he / she / it / we / they didn't arrive late.
  I / you / he / she / it / we / they didn't go home.
- **To make questions, we put *did* before the subject. We can also use question words.**
  Did I / you / he / she / it / we / they arrive late?
  Where did I / you / he / she / it / we / they go?

**3 Make the affirmative sentences negative. Use the simple past.**

1 They finished class at ten o'clock.
They didn't finish class at ten o'clock.
2 He sang a song in the school concert.
........ .
3 I copied the words into my notebook.
........ .
4 The *Titanic* sank in the Pacific Ocean.
........ .
5 They chatted online yesterday.
........ .
6 You bought a computer last week.
........ .

**4 Rewrite the questions. Use the simple past.**

1 leg / When / Michael / his / break / did / ?
When did Michael break his leg ?
2 change / Tina / hair / Did / her / ?
........ ?
3 they / Italian / did / When / learn / ?
........ ?
4 into / car / Did / tree / the / crash / the / ?
........ ?
5 study / boys / Where / did / the / ?
........ ?
6 last / you / have / Did / party / week / a / ?
........ ?


Workbook p.W6

# 1 My time

## Introducing the topic

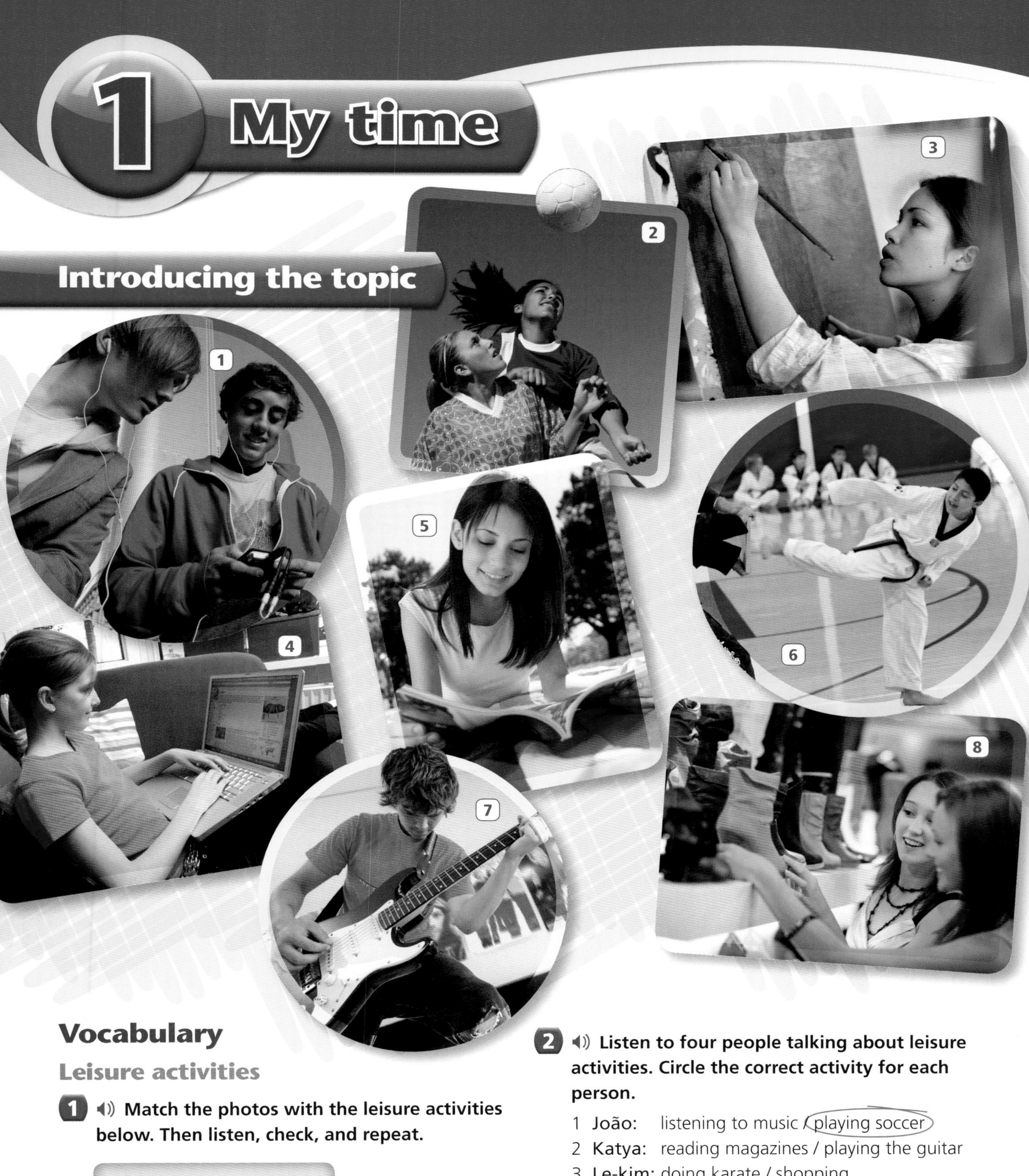

## Vocabulary

### Leisure activities

**1** **Match the photos with the leisure activities below. Then listen, check, and repeat.**

- 6 doing karate
- ☐ listening to music
- ☐ painting
- ☐ playing soccer
- ☐ playing the guitar
- ☐ reading magazines
- ☐ shopping
- ☐ using the computer

**2** **Listen to four people talking about leisure activities. Circle the correct activity for each person.**

1 **João:** listening to music / playing soccer
2 **Katya:** reading magazines / playing the guitar
3 **Le-kim:** doing karate / shopping
4 **Sandra:** painting / using the computer

**3** **Write sentences about leisure activities. Use the words below.**

awful boring exciting fun interesting OK

*Doing karate is fun, but running is boring.*

# Exploring the topic

## Friend finder

Do you want to make friends in other countries? Try **Friend Finder**!

### Lien

Hi! My name is Lien. I'm from Hai Phong, Vietnam. I'm fifteen years old, and I'm in high school. I love painting, and I also enjoy reading. Swimming and going to the beach are fun, too. I don't like playing soccer, and I hate running. Running is awful!

**Make friends** Chat 

### Emilio

Hello. My name is Emilio. I'm fourteen years old, and I live in Carúpano, Venezuela. I'm in 8th grade. I love playing soccer. It's my favorite sport! Listening to music is fun, but I don't like singing. My voice is terrible, and my friends laugh at me!

**Make friends** Chat 

### Kostas

Hi! My name is Kostas. I'm sixteen years old, and I live in Thessaloniki, Greece. I'm in 9th grade at school. I love playing computer games. I think they're awesome! I also like painting. I don't do a lot of sports, but I think playing basketball is fun. What do you think?

**Make friends** Chat 

### Alicia

Hey! My name is Alicia. I'm fifteen years old, and I live in Porto Alegre, Brazil. I love going to the beach! I also like skateboarding, and I enjoy listening to music. My favorite singer is Rihanna. I hate shopping! It's so boring!

**Make friends** Chat 

## Reading

**1 Read the profiles quickly. Check (✓) the information that appears in the profiles.**

name ☑ dislikes ☐ likes ☐
family ☐ age ☐ appearance ☐

**2 Read and listen to the profiles again. Fill in the blanks with the names of the people.**

1 Lien loves painting and reading.
2 ________ enjoys playing soccer.
3 ________ likes skateboarding.
4 ________ enjoys playing computer games.
5 ________ hates running.
6 ________ doesn't enjoy shopping.
7 ________ doesn't like singing.
8 ________ and ________ like going to the beach.

**3 Complete the sentences with your opinions about leisure activities.**

1 I like ________.
2 I love ________.
3 I think ________ is OK.
4 I don't like ________.
5 I hate ________.

# Grammar

## Gerunds (*-ing* form)

Talking about likes and dislikes

**1 Look at the chart.**

| *like / enjoy / love / don't like / hate* + *-ing* form | | |
|---|---|---|
| I / You / We / They | **love**<br>**don't like** | play**ing** tennis. |
| He / She / It | **enjoys**<br>**doesn't like** | read**ing** magazines. |

**2 Put ☺ by the positive sentences and ☹ by the negative sentences.**

1 Kim doesn't like playing soccer. ☹
2 You enjoy reading magazines.
3 Their parents hate running.
4 Susie loves shopping on Saturdays.
5 Tom and Sam like playing baseball.
6 My friends and I don't like climbing.

### Take note!

**Spelling rules for *-ing* forms**

- **Regular: add *-ing***
  read ➜ reading
- **Consonant + *-e*: ~~-e~~ + *-ing***
  ride ➜ riding
- **One vowel + one consonant: double the consonant + *-ing***
  run ➜ running

**3 Fill in the blanks with the *-ing* form of the verbs below.**

do play read ~~ride~~ run shop

1 John loves *riding* .......... his mountain bike.
2 I don't like .......... soccer.
3 We love .......... . Buying new clothes is fun!
4 Carla enjoys .......... books about science.
5 Evan and Tania like .......... in marathons.
6 Do you like .......... homework?

**4 Look at the chart.**

| *-ing* form + *be* + adjective | |
|---|---|
| Running | is boring. |
| Playing soccer | is exciting. |

**5 Look at the pictures. Write sentences.**

1 *Playing tennis is hard* .
2 .......... .
3 .......... .
4 .......... .
5 .......... .
6 .......... .

Puzzle page 83, puzzle 1A

**6 Over to you!**

**Write two true sentences and one false sentence. Use the verbs *like*, *enjoy*, *love*, and *hate*. Can your classmates guess the false sentence?**

Student A: I love reading. I like running. I hate listening to music.
Student B: Sentence 3 is false.
Student A: You're right. / You're wrong.

# Building the topic

Alex: I have to (1) *wash* the *dishes*. I hate it! And my sister? She has to (2) ______ her ______, but she likes doing that. I don't understand her!

Betty: I have to (3) ______ my ______. It isn't fun! My dad has to (4) ______ ______ the ______. It smells terrible!

Paul: I have to (5) ______ the ______. My sister doesn't have to help me, but she has to (6) ______ ______ her ______. She has a lot of clothes!

Tina: I have to (7) ______ ______ for my little brother. He's always hungry! My mom has to (8) ______ the ______. It's hard work!

## Vocabulary

### Chores at home

**1** **Look at the pictures and fill in the blanks with the words below. Then listen, check, and repeat.**

| | |
|---|---|
| clean (your) room | put away (your) clothes |
| cut the grass | set the table |
| make lunch | take out the garbage |
| make (your) bed | ~~wash the dishes~~ |

**2** **Fill in the chart with the correct chore from exercise 1.**

| | |
|---|---|
| **bedroom** | *make your bed;* |
| **dining room** | |
| **kitchen** | |
| **yard** | |

**3** **Read the sentences. Write the name of the person.**

1 He has to take out the garbage. *Betty's dad*
2 She has to make lunch for her brother. ______
3 He has to wash the dishes. ______
4 She has to make her bed. ______
5 She doesn't have to set the table. ______
6 She has to cut the grass. ______
7 She has to put away her clothes. ______
8 She has to clean her room. ______

# Grammar

## *have to*

Talking about obligations

**1 Look at the chart.**

| Obligation | No obligation |
|---|---|
| I / You **have to** set the table. | I / You **don't have to** wash the dishes. |
| He / She / It **has to** cut the grass. | He / She / It **doesn't have to** make lunch. |
| We / You / They **have to** wash the dishes. | We / You / They **don't have to** set the table. |
| **Questions** | **Short answers** |
| **Do** you **have to** do chores? | Yes, I **do**. / No, I **don't**. |
| **Does** he / she **have to** do chores? | Yes, he / she **does**.<br>No, he / she **doesn't**. |

**2 Circle the correct word.**

1 My brother **have** / **has** to clean his room.
2 Leo's dad **have** / **has** to cut the grass.
3 You **have** / **has** to put away your things.
4 I **have** / **has** to set the table on Sundays.
5 My parents **have** / **has** to take out the garbage.
6 My sister **have** / **has** to make her bed.

**3 Fill in the blanks with *have to* / *has to* (✓) or *don't have to* / *doesn't have to* (✗).**

1 A doctor has to help sick people. (✓)

2 A singer ............ ............ wear a uniform. (✗)

3 Teachers ............ ............ like working with children. (✓)

4 Models ............ ............ look fashionable. (✗)

5 Airline pilots ............ ............ serve coffee. (✗)

6 A mechanic ............ ............ fix cars. (✓)

**4 Look at the poster. Write sentences.**

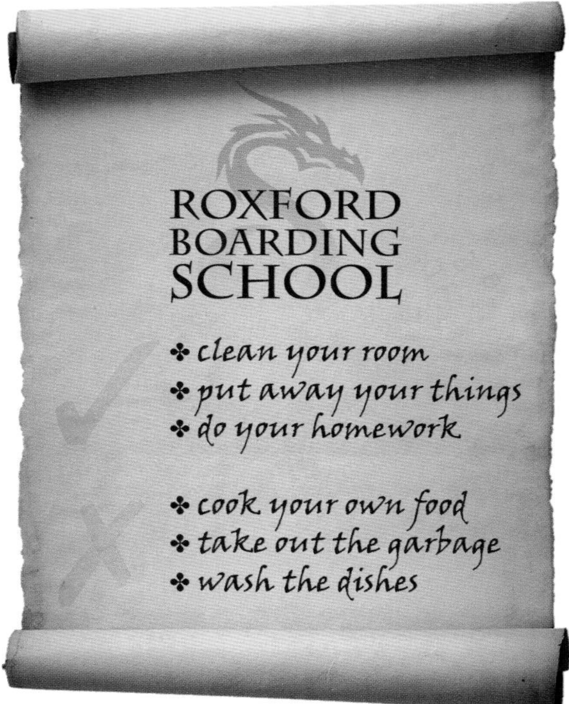


1 You have to clean your room.
2 ............................................ .
3 ............................................ .
4 ............................................ .
5 ............................................ .
6 ............................................ .

**Puzzle** page 83, puzzle 1B

**5 Over to you!**

**Write three chores that you have to do at home. Ask your partner.**

Student A: Do you have to make your bed?
Student B: Yes, I do. / No, I don't.

Living English

# Acting School

Julie Darnell is sixteen years old, and she loves acting. It's her passion! Julie goes to a special high school for drama students in Houston, Texas. This is her typical day.

In the morning, Julie has to study normal school subjects. Her favorite subject is art because she enjoys painting and drawing pictures. Julie is also good at science, geography, and Spanish, but she doesn't like history. "Learning all those names and dates is hard!" she says.

In the afternoon, Julie and her classmates have acting classes. It isn't easy because they have to remember a lot of dialogues.

On Wednesdays, Julie has singing and dancing classes. "I really want to act in musicals, like *Phantom of the Opera* and *Chicago*, so I have to sing and dance well, too," she says.

In her free time, Julie likes playing the piano and watching TV. Her favorite show is *Glee*, but she also likes *Gossip Girl*.

In the evening, Julie is often tired, but she has to do her homework before she goes to bed. Julie likes studying hard. "I'm making my dreams come true," she says.

*Julie in acting class*

## Reading

**1 Look at the Reading skills box.**

**Reading skills**

Getting a general idea

- **When you first read a text, read it quickly to understand the general idea.**

**2 Read the article. Answer the questions.**

1 Does Julie go to a regular high school?

........................................................

2 Does Julie like her school?

........................................................

**3 Read again. Circle T (True) or F (False).**

1 Singing is Julie's passion. T / (F)
2 She has acting classes in the morning. T / F
3 History isn't Julie's favorite subject. T / F
4 She has singing classes on Mondays. T / F
5 Julie watches TV in her free time. T / F
6 She can't play a musical instrument. T / F

**4 Answer the questions.**

1 Where does Julie go to school?
in Houston, Texas

2 Why doesn't she like studying history?

........................................................

3 When does Julie have her acting classes?

........................................................

4 Why does she taking singing classes?

........................................................

5 What's Julie's favorite TV show?

........................................................

6 Why does Julie study hard?

........................................................


Workbook p.W12

## Listening

### New friends

**1** Listen to the conversation. What is Mike's and Deb's favorite activity?

**2** Listen again. Circle the correct words.

1 Mike is from New York City / New Jersey.
2 For Mike, the town is **boring / small**.
3 The people in town are very **friendly / happy**.
4 Mike likes playing the **guitar / piano** in his free time.
5 Deb goes to a **tennis / basketball** club in town.
6 Deb **has to / doesn't have to** do a lot of homework.

**3** Fill in the blanks with the words below. Then listen and check.

~~different~~ homework hours like love there

1 Wow! It's very *different* here for you, I guess.
2 I ______ playing tennis.
3 Maybe we can go ______ together some time.
4 Cool! And do students have to do a lot of ______ here?
5 No, just one or two ______ a day. It's not too bad.
6 I think I ______ this school.

## Speaking

### Talking about likes and dislikes

**1** Listen and read.

Jordan: What kind of music do you like?
Chester: I like rock music.
Jordan: What are you listening to right now?
Chester: I'm listening to Green Day. They're awesome.

Jordan: What kind of books do you like?
Mariella: I like science fiction books.
Jordan: What are you reading right now?
Mariella: I'm reading *Space Adventure*. It's exciting.

**2** Look at the Pronunciation box. Listen to the examples. Then listen again and repeat.

**Pronunciation**

Sentence stress
- **We usually stress verbs, nouns, and question words.**
  What kind of music do you like?
  I like rock music.

**3** Listen. Circle the stressed word(s) in each sentence. Then listen again and repeat.

1 Where do you live?
2 I'm a student.
3 I like swimming.
4 What kind of books do you like?

**4** Practice the dialogues in exercise 1.

**5** Now change the words in blue. Write new dialogues. Then practice the dialogues in class.

# Round-up

## Writing

### A personal profile

**1** **Look at the Writing skills box.**

> **Writing skills**
> Paragraphs
> - **Develop one main idea in each paragraph.**

**2** **Read the profile. Match the paragraphs with the ideas below.**

usual activities 2
personal information ......
likes and dislikes ......

**(1)** Hi there! My name is Marie, but my nickname on the Internet is India. I'm sixteen years old, and I go to Atlantic High School, in Elizabeth, New Jersey, in the United States.

**(2)** On school days, I get up early, walk to school, and then I talk with my friends before class. After school, I often go swimming, or I ride my bike. I love doing sports! At home, I have to do my homework, put away my things, and take Max out. He's my dog!

**(3)** In my free time, I like reading fashion magazines. I think they're interesting! I also enjoy listening to hip-hop music. Right now, I'm listening to a group called The Cool Kids. I don't like watching TV. I think it's boring!

**3** **Complete the chart with information about Marie.**

| **Personal information** | |
|---|---|
| Name ...... | Country ...... |
| Nickname ...... | Town ...... |
| Age ...... | |
| **Usual activities** | |
| In the morning, I *get up early, walk to school, and then talk with my friends before class.* | |
| After school, I | |
| At home, I have to | |
| **Likes and dislikes** | |
| I like | |
| I don't like | |
| I think | |

**4** **Make a chart with information about you.**

**5** **Write your profile. Use the profile in exercise 1 and your chart to help you.**

## I can ...

**1** **Write sentences describing your likes and dislikes. Use *like / don't like / love / enjoy + -ing*.**

1 *I love buying new clothes* .
2 ...... .
3 ...... .
4 ...... .

**I can describe personal likes and dislikes.**
Yes, I can. ☐ I need more practice. ☐

**2** **Fill in the blanks with *have to / has to / don't have to / doesn't have to*.**

1 My brother *has to* do his homework.
2 I ...... study every day.
3 We ...... clean our bedrooms every day.
4 My teacher ...... get up at six o'clock in the morning.

**I can talk about obligations.**
Yes, I can. ☐ I need more practice. ☐

# 2 Get moving!

## Introducing the topic

1 train

2

3

4

5

6

7

8

9

10

## Vocabulary

### Transportation

**1** **Label the photos with the words below. Then listen, check, and repeat.**

airplane bus canoe car ferry helicopter motorcycle sailboat subway ~~train~~

**2** **Complete the chart with the words in exercise 1.**

| | |
|---|---|
| **Land** | bus; |
| **Water** | |
| **Air** | |

**Take note!**

- **We use the preposition *by* to talk about the kinds of transportation that we use.**
  Some people go to work by train.
  **But:** I go to work on foot.

**3** **Fill in the blanks with kinds of transportation.**

1 You can travel under the city by subway.
2 One or two people can travel very fast by ______.
3 Cars and people can travel on water by ______.
4 You can travel through the air from one country to another by ______.
5 You can travel on water, using the wind to move, by ______.

Workbook p.W14 → MultiROM

## Exploring the topic

# South American Express!

Are you and a friend looking for some excitement? Enter our South American Express competition and win $10,000. Here are the rules for contestants!

### Rules:

- You have to visit every capital city in South America in 60 days.
- You can't travel alone. You have to stay with your friend all the time.
- You can travel between six o'clock in the morning and eight o'clock in the evening.
- Each person can spend $10 a day on food, transportation, and a place to sleep.

### Transportation:

You can travel in many different ways, but there is one important rule. You can't use any transportation with a motor!

**On land:** You can travel on foot or ride a bike. You can also ride a horse! You can't go by car, subway, bus, or train.

**On water:** You can travel on water by canoe or sailboat, but you can't go by ferry or motorboat!

**In the air:** You can't travel by airplane or by helicopter, but you can fly in a hot air balloon. It doesn't have a motor!

**Enter now and start traveling!**

## Reading

**1** Read and listen to the article. How many kinds of transportation can you find?

**2** Read again. Circle T (True) or F (False).

1 Contestants can travel alone. T / (F)
2 They can travel by ferry. T / F
3 Contestants can't travel at night. T / F
4 They have three months to travel. T / F
5 Contestants can win $10,000. T / F
6 They can't use air transportation. T / F

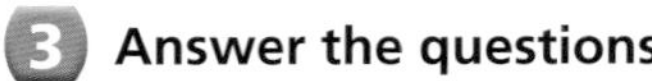

**3** Answer the questions.

1 What places do contestants have to visit?
*the capital cities of South America*

2 What time can they start traveling every day?

3 What can't contestants travel by in the air?

4 How much money can each person spend?

5 What kinds of land transportation can they use?

## Grammar

### *can / can't*

Talking about rules

**1 Look at the chart.**

| **Affirmative** | |
|---|---|
| I / You / We / They / He / She / It **can** park here. | |
| **Negative** | |
| I / You / We / They / He / She / It **can't** park here. | |
| **Questions** | **Short answers** |
| **Can** we **park** here? | Yes, you **can**.<br>No, you **can't**. |

**Take note!**

- **We also use *can / can't* to talk about rules.**
  People can use their cell phones on the bus.
  You can't park your motorcycles there.

**2 Fill in the blanks with *can* or *can't*.**

1 Phil *can't* .......... park there.
2 Emily .......... park there for two hours.

3 They .......... skateboard on the sidewalk.
4 We .......... skateboard at the skatepark.

5 I .......... go scuba diving at that beach.
6 We .......... go swimming in that area.

**3 Look at the advertisement for a lion safari tour. Write questions with *can* and *can't*. Then answer the questions.**

1 Can you bring food and drinks?
*Yes, you can* .
2 .......... get out of the bus?
.......... .
3 .......... ?
.......... .
4 .......... ?
.......... .
5 .......... ?
.......... .
6 .......... ?
.......... .

Puzzle page 83, puzzle 2A

**4 Over to you!**

**Do you have to follow a lot of rules at home? Write two sentences with *can* and two sentences with *can't*. Then compare with a classmate.**

Student A: I can't stay out after 10 p.m. Can you?
Student B: Yes, I can.
Student A: I can get a piercing. Can you?
Student B: No, I can't.

# Building the topic

1 The bus isn't fast enough.

2 The test was too ........ .

3 It is very ........ in the library.

4 That boat isn't ........ enough.

5 The airplane is ........ .

6 Her homework is too ........ .

7 The bus is too ........ .

8 The traffic is too ........ .

9 The train is too ........ .

10 That bridge is too ........ .

## Vocabulary

### Opposite adjectives

**1** **Look at the pictures. Fill in the blanks with the words below. Then listen, check, and repeat.**

comfortable dangerous difficult easy ~~fast~~
noisy quiet safe slow uncomfortable

**2** **Look at the adjectives in exercise 1. Write five pairs of opposites.**

1 fast ◄► slow
2 ........ ◄► ........
3 ........ ◄► ........
4 ........ ◄► ........
5 ........ ◄► ........

**3** **Circle the correct word.**

1 I hate motorcycles! They're too **easy** / **noisy**!
2 Don't use that old bike. It isn't **difficult** / **safe** enough.
3 We never travel by bus. It's too **slow** / **comfortable**.
4 The subway isn't **noisy** / **fast** enough. Let's take a taxi.
5 A helicopter ride? No, thanks! It's too **dangerous** / **quiet**.

**4** **Write five pairs of sentences with opposite adjectives.**

*English is easy. Science is difficult.*

## Grammar

### *too / not … enough*

Talking about problems

**1 Look at the chart.**

| *too* + adjective | *not* + adjective + *enough* |
|---|---|
| It's **too** dangerous. | It is**n't** safe **enough**. |

**2 Match the sentences with same meaning.**

1 It's too easy. — c
2 It isn't fast enough.
3 It's too dangerous.
4 It isn't quiet enough.
5 It's too uncomfortable.

a It isn't comfortable enough.
b It's too noisy.
c It isn't difficult enough.
d It's too slow.
e It isn't safe enough.

**3 Fill in the blanks with *too* and the adjectives below.**

cold difficult expensive ~~loud~~ fast

1 Turn down that music! It's *too loud* !
2 This bike costs $1,000. It's ______ .
3 I can't do this exercise. It's ______ .
4 Motorcycles are dangerous. They're ______ .
5 They don't like winter. It's ______ .

**4 Look at the poster. Write sentences with *be + not … enough* and the adjectives in parentheses.**

1 Paul wants to race. He's only sixteen. (old)
He *isn't old enough* .
2 Julie's height is 1.45 m. (tall)
She ______ .
3 Kuan's bike is very slow. (fast)
It ______ .
4 Adam only weighs 60 kg. (heavy)
He ______ .
5 Naomi's bike is 20 years old. (new)
It ______ .

**5 Look at the pictures. Write sentences with *be + too* or *not … enough*.**

1 The car *is too* small. (small)
2 The beach ______ . (sunny)
3 Her umbrella ______ . (big)
4 He ______ . (tall)
5 The suitcase ______ . (heavy)
6 The ocean ______ . (warm)

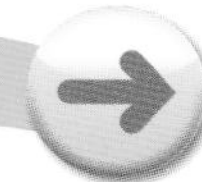
Puzzle page 83, puzzle 2B

**6 Over to you!**

**Write about things you don't like. Give reasons with *too* and *not … enough*. Then tell a classmate.**

Student A: I don't like reading comic books.
Student B: Why not?
Student A: I think they're too boring.

Workbook p.W17 → MultiROM

## Living English

Are you going to travel around the U.S.? Do you want your dog or cat to come with you? Try Pet Airways. It's the country's first airline for pets!

Traveling by air is a problem for some pet owners. They can't take their dogs and cats in the main part of the airplane. There isn't enough room, so pets usually have to travel in the cargo hold, with people's baggage. Some pet owners worry that it's too cold and noisy in the cargo hold, and some pets get nervous.

At Pet Airways, dogs and cats aren't baggage! They can travel like first-class passengers. Two hours before the flight, owners leave their pets in a waiting area. During the flight, the animals are safe and comfortable, because they travel in the main part of the airplane.

**Frequently Asked Questions**

**Q: Where does Pet Airways fly?**
A: It flies between many large cities, like New York, Los Angeles, and Chicago.

**Q: How much does a typical Pet Airways flight cost?**
A: A flight from New York to Los Angeles costs about $250.

**Q: Can people fly in the airplane with their pets?**
A: No, they can't. There aren't any seats for people!

## Reading

**1 Read the advertisement quickly. Can people travel on Pet Airways airplanes?**

**2 Read again. Fill in the blanks.**

1 Pet Airways is an *airline* ______ for pets.
2 On normal airplanes, pets have to travel in the ______.
3 The animals stay in a ______ before the flight.
4 Pets travel in the ______ part of Pet Airways airplanes.
5 Pet Airways flies between many ______ cities in the U.S.

**3 Answer the questions.**

1 What kinds of animals does Pet Airways carry?
*cats and dogs*
2 Why can't animals stay with their owners on a normal airplane?
______
3 Why don't owners want to leave their pets in the hold?
______
4 When can you leave your pet in the waiting area?
______
5 How much does a typical flight cost?
______

 Workbook p.W18

## Listening

### At the transportation museum

1 Look at the Listening skills box.

**Listening skills**

Listening for key words

- Key words are usually nouns, verbs, and adjectives. They can help you understand when you are listening.

2 Kevin is talking to a guide at the museum. Listen for the key words below. Who says these words? Write them in the chart.

café drink DVD gift shop open ~~questions~~ videos visit

| | |
|---|---|
| Kevin | questions; |
| The guide | |

3 Listen to the conversation again. Then answer the questions.

1 Can people take photos in the museum?
No, they can't .

2 Can they buy a DVD in the gift shop?
.

3 Can visitors touch some of the exhibits?
.

4 Can visitors take food into the museum?
.

5 Can people visit the museum on Sundays?
.

## Speaking

### Talking about rules

1 Listen and read.

Police officer: Excuse me. You can't leave your bike here.
Mariella: Oh! I'm sorry! Where can I leave it?
Police officer: You can leave it over there.

Museum guide: Excuse me. You can't use your cell phone in the museum.
Mariella: I'm sorry. I didn't know.
Museum guide: It's OK. You can use it outside.

2 Look at the Pronunciation box. Listen to the examples. Then listen again and repeat.

**Pronunciation**

Weak vowels (*can* / *can't*)

- The vowel in *can* is weak in affirmative sentences. We don't stress it.
  You can use your cell phone.
- The vowel in *can't* is strong. We stress it.
  You can't use your cell phone.

3 Listen. Are the underlined words stressed or unstressed? Write S or U.

1 We <u>can</u> stay out late tonight. U
2 You <u>can't</u> park your car there. ……
3 <u>Can</u> you go to Mike's party? ……
4 Where <u>can</u> I take photos? ……
5 You <u>can't</u> go swimming in the lake. ……

4 Practice the dialogues in exercise 1.

5 Now change the words in blue. Write new dialogues. Then practice the dialogues in class.

# Round-up

## Writing

### An e-mail about a trip

**1** **Read the e-mail. What was Maggie's favorite place in Toronto?**

**2** **Fill in the chart with information about Maggie's trip.**

| My trip | |
|---|---|
| Where and when did she go? | Toronto, last month |
| Who traveled with her? | |
| How did they travel to Toronto? | |
| Was there a problem? | |
| What was her favorite place? | |
| What can people do there? | |
| What other place did she like? | |
| What can / can't you do there? | |
| Did they have a good time? | |

**3** **Make a chart for a trip you took in the past. Use the questions in exercise 2 to help you. Write an e-mail to a friend about your trip.**

Hi, Trevor,

Paul and I were in Toronto for five days last month. We traveled by train from New York City. The train was comfortable, but the trip was too long. It took 11 hours!

When we arrived in Toronto, we visited the city on foot, and by subway or bus. It was really easy! There are a lot of things to see in Toronto, but my favorite place was a tall building called the CN Tower. It's 553 m tall! Tourists can go up the tower and take photos, but they have to buy a ticket first.

I also loved the Toronto Islands. They have beaches, but the water is sometimes too cold to swim. It only takes about 15 minutes to get to the islands by ferry. You can't drive a car on the islands, but you can rent a bike. It's a great way to get around!

Paul and I had a really great time in Toronto, but one week wasn't long enough to see everything!

Love,

Maggie

## I can ...

**1** **Write sentences about rules at your school. Use *can* and *can't*.**

1 You can't arrive late.
2 ______ drink in the classroom.
3 ______ bring your cell phone to school.
4 ______ listen to music in the break.

**I can talk about rules.**
Yes, I can. ☐ I need more practice. ☐

**2** **Fill in the blanks with *be* + *too* or *not ... enough*.**

1 You can't travel alone. You are too young.
2 She's only fifteen. She ______ old ______ to drive a car.
3 There are eight people. This car ______ small for them.
4 Kiki is only 1.40 m. He ______ tall ______ to play basketball.

**I can talk about problems.**
Yes, I can. ☐ I need more practice. ☐

# A Review

## Vocabulary

### Leisure activities

**1** **Fill in the blanks with the correct leisure activities.**

1 Juan loves playing soccer .
2 Eun-ju thinks ............ is cool.
3 Keira enjoys ............ .
4 Jung doesn't like ............ .
5 Pedro loves ............ .
6 Ana thinks ............ is boring.
7 Lisa enjoys ............ .
8 For Tomoki, ............ is exciting.

### Chores at home

**2** **Label the pictures of the chores.**

1 put away

2 ............

3 ............

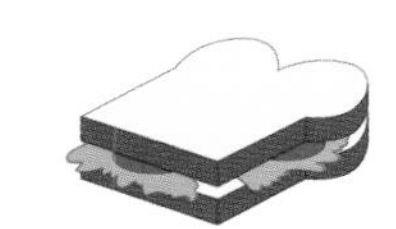

4 ............

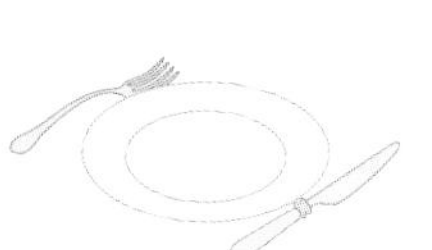

5 ............

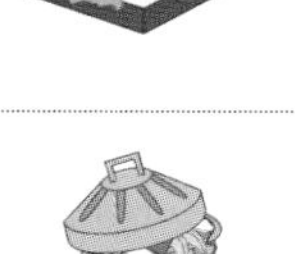

6 ............

7 ............

8 ............

### Transportation

**3** **Unscramble the letters and write the kinds of transportation.**

1 u b s
bus

2 e r o c m t c o y l
............

3 y e r f r
............

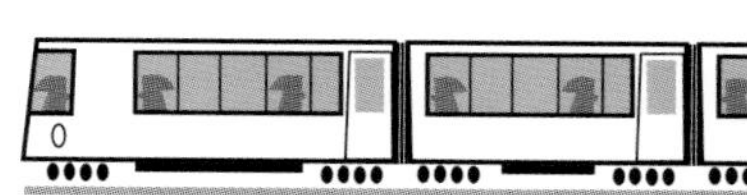

4 i r t n a
............

5 b s o a t l i a
............

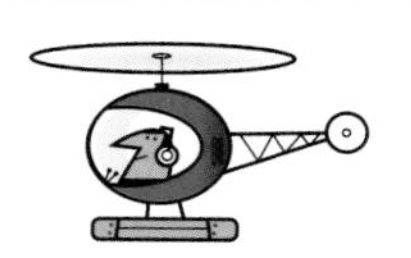

6 c e r p h l i o t e
............

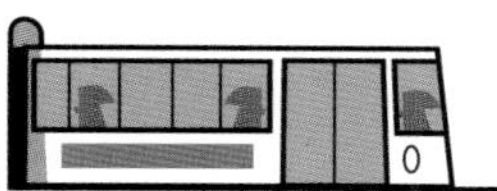

7 a u y s b w
............

8 n e a l p r i a
............

9 a n o e c
............

10 r c a
............

### Opposite adjectives

**4** **Circle the adjective in each sentence. Then write the opposite.**

1 We went on a very (fast) train.
slow
2 Why are you being so noisy today?
............
3 Is this sofa new? It's comfortable.
............
4 I think math is a difficult subject.
............
5 Do you think motorcycles are safe?
............

# Review

## Grammar

### Gerunds (-*ing* form)

**1 Write sentences about Justin Bieber's likes and dislikes.**

1 enjoy / spend time with his friends
He enjoys spending time with his friends.
2 love / sing ______
______.
3 like / watch movies ______
______.
4 not like / do homework ______
______.
5 enjoy / help other people ______
______.
6 love / listen to music ______
______.

### *have to*

**2 Fill in the blanks with *have to, has to, don't have to,* or *doesn't have to.***

1 I'm a student. I have to study, but I don't have to teach.
2 They're actors. They ______ learn lines. They ______ write movies.
3 She's a chef. She ______ wash the dishes. She ______ make food.
4 He's an inventor. He ______ work in an office. He ______ create things.
5 We're athletes. We ______ run every day. We ______ use a computer.
6 You're a doctor. You ______ work with people. You ______ work with animals.

### *can / can't*

**3 Write sentences about the Metropolitan Museum of Art with *can / can't.***

1 You can't take photos.
(take photos ✗)
2 ______.
(bring food and drink ✓)
3 ______.
(touch the exhibits ✗)
4 ______.
(go there on Sundays ✓)
5 ______.
(carry large bags ✗)
6 ______.
(go for free ✓)

### *too / not … enough*

**4 Fill in the blanks with *too* or *not … enough* and the adjectives in parentheses.**

1 We can't use that canoe. It isn't safe enough. (safe)
2 They don't want to take the bus. It's ______. (slow)
3 Dan's eighteen. He isn't ______ (old) to drive a car.
4 I did the test in ten minutes. It was ______. (easy)
5 The spaghetti is ______ (hot). It has to cool down.
6 This chair isn't ______ (comfortable) for me.

## Study skills

**Using your coursebook**

*Engage* has different types of material to help you study.

**1 Where can you find these things?**

1 "I want to know how many units are in this book."
Pages 2 and 3
2 "I want to find a list of the vocabulary in Unit 2."
Workbook page ______
3 "I want to do a puzzle related to Unit 2."
Page ______
4 "I want to study grammar explanations for Unit 2."
Workbook page ______

**2 Now find the answers to these questions about the coursebook.**

1 How many Review units are in this book? 4
2 Which unit teaches us the names of sports? ______
3 How many puzzles does each unit have? ______
4 Which unit teaches us about the past progressive? ______

# 3 Crime scene

## Introducing the topic

2 ..................

5 ..................

## Vocabulary

### Conflict verbs

**1** **Match the photos with the words below. Then listen, check, and repeat.**

argue ~~complain~~ fight hide hit shout

**2** **Circle the correct word.**

1 My cat likes to **shout** / **hide** under the bed.
2 David **hit** / **argued** his sister with a ball.
3 They always **complain** / **fight** about the cold weather.
4 I **shout** / **fight** loudly when our soccer team wins a game.
5 We **hit** / **complain** when the bus is late.
6 Kris and Matt **argue** / **hide** a lot. They never agree!

**3** **Are these sentences true or false for you?**

1 I complain when people are late. T / F
2 We often shout in the classroom. T / F
3 I sometimes fight with my brother / sister. T / F
4 I never argue with my parents. T / F
5 I hide in my room when I'm sad. T / F

Workbook p.W20 → MultiROM

# Exploring the topic

## Reading

**1 Look at the picture. Match the words with objects a–f.**

1 gun c  
2 knife ……  
3 bag ……  
4 sidewalk ……  
5 umbrella ……  
6 store ……

**Witness A**

It was six fifteen, and I was at the bus stop. Two men were standing next to a black car on the street. They were fighting, and one of the men had a gun. There was a green car at the corner. A young woman was standing next to a bag on the sidewalk. She was taking a photo with her camera.

**Witness B**

I was driving down the street at about six fifteen. Two men were arguing on the street corner, next to a blue car. On the other side of the street, there was a bag on the sidewalk. A young man was looking inside the bag. He had a camera. There was a woman at the bus stop with an umbrella.

**Witness C**

I was closing my store at six fifteen. Two men were standing on the street corner next to a blue car and they were shouting. One of the men had a knife. A woman was looking inside a bag on the sidewalk. There was a gun next to the bag. Another woman was hiding around the corner. There was a woman at the bus stop with an umbrella.

**2 Read and listen to the three witness statements. Which statement matches the picture exactly?**

**3 Read the correct statement again. Answer the questions.**

1 What was the old man closing?  
his store

2 Where were the two men shouting?  
……

3 What was one of the men holding?  
……

4 What was next to the bag?  
……

5 Who was hiding around a corner?  
……

6 Where was the woman with the umbrella?  
……

# Grammar

## Past progressive (affirmative / negative)

Talking about actions in progress in the past

**1 Look at the chart.**

| Affirmative | Negative |
|---|---|
| I **was** talking. | I **wasn't** shouting. |
| You **were** running. | You **weren't** walking. |
| He / She / It **was** hiding. | He / She / It **wasn't** fighting. |
| We / You / They **were** arguing. | We / You / They **weren't** talking. |

**2 Circle the correct form.**

It was four o'clock. The sun (1) **wasn't / weren't** shining. It (2) **was / were** raining. Elisa and Terri (3) **was / were** waiting for the bus, but they (4) **wasn't / weren't** waiting on the sidewalk. They (5) **was / were** standing inside the bus shelter because it (6) **was / were** raining.

**3 Complete the dialogue. Use the correct form of the verbs in parentheses.**

Teacher: What was the problem during math class today, boys?
Victor: Alex (1) was talking (talk).
Alex: That isn't true! I (2) ________ (not talk). I (3) ________ (read).
Victor: You (4) ________ (not read). Your book was closed!
Alex: Well, you (5) ________ (send) a text message. I saw you!
Victor: I (6) ________ (not send) a text message! My cell phone was in my bag.
Teacher: Well, I (7) ________ (not watch), so I don't know what happened. Let's forget it, OK?

**4 What were the people doing at 6 p.m. yesterday? Write affirmative or negative sentences. Use the words in parentheses.**

1 The man was talking (talk) on the phone.
2 The old woman ________ (sleep).
3 The girls ________ (watch) TV.
4 The old man ________ (eat) dinner.
5 The woman ________ (dance).
6 The boys ________ (play) a game.

Puzzle page 85, puzzle 3A

**5 Over to you!**

**Write two true and one false sentence about yesterday. Use the affirmative and negative past progressive. Can the class guess which sentence is false?**

Student A: At 6 p.m. yesterday, I was doing my homework. I wasn't having dinner at eight o'clock. I was watching TV at eight thirty.
Student B: Sentence two is false.
Student A: No, it's true.
Student B: Sentence three is false.
Student A: Yes, it's false. I was reading at eight thirty.

# Building the topic

## Vocabulary

### Places in a street

**1** **Look at the pictures. Fill in the blanks with the words below. Then listen, check, and repeat.**

> apartment ~~bank~~ fire escape garage
> police station street corner

**2** **The police are interviewing Ellen, Jason, and Mark. Listen to the interviews. Who is telling the truth? Who is lying?**

**3** **Circle T (True) or F (False).**

1 Jason and Mark were robbing the bank on April 8th at 3:50 p.m. T / (F)
2 On April 6th, at 4:50 p.m., Mark was at Ellen's apartment. T / F
3 Jason and Mark were going to get the money from Ellen. T / F
4 Ellen was on the fire escape at 6:10 p.m. T / F
5 Jason was angry because Mark crashed his car. T / F

# Grammar

## Past progressive (questions)

Asking about actions in progress in the past

**1** **Look at the chart.**

| ***yes / no* questions** | **Answers** |
|---|---|
| **Was** I shouting? | Yes, I **was**. / No, I **wasn't**. |
| **Were** you complaining? | Yes, you **were**.<br>No, you **weren't**. |
| **Was** he / she / it running? | Yes, he / she / it **was**.<br>No, he / she / it **wasn't**. |
| **Were** we / you / they fighting? | Yes, we / you / they **were**.<br>No, we / you / they **weren't**. |
| ***Wh-* questions** | |
| Where **was** she going? | She **was** going to the movies. |
| What **were** they doing? | They **were** doing their homework. |

**2** **Put the words in order to make questions.**

1 were / What / at / doing / five o'clock / you / ?
What were you doing at five o'clock ?

2 to / Was / he / night / talking / Marcy / last / ?
?

3 they / What / last / watching / Saturday / were / ?
?

4 morning / was / she / Where / yesterday / going / ?
?

5 they / afternoon / Why / running / were / this / ?
?

6 she / week / arguing / Was / with Tom / last / ?
?

**3** **Match the answers with the questions in exercise 2.**

1 They were watching a sports show on TV. 3
2 Yes, he was.
3 I was playing soccer with my friends.
4 They were training for the marathon.
5 Yes, she was.
6 She was going to the library for a book.

**4** **Write the questions. Use the underlined parts of the answers to help you.**

1 What were you looking for ?
I was looking for <u>my history book</u>.

2 ?
Tyler was running <u>because he was late</u>.

3 ?
They were waiting for us <u>outside the mall</u>.

4 ?
He was watching <u>the evening news</u>.

5 ?
Julia was going <u>to the movie theater</u>.

6 ?
I was having lunch <u>at 1 p.m.</u>?

**Puzzle** page 85, puzzle 3B

**5** **Over to you!**

**Look at the strange activities below. Ask and answer questions about why you were doing these activities. Think of a good answer!**

carry a monkey climb on the roof
dance in your classroom
read in the shower sing in the street

Student A: Why were you carrying a monkey yesterday?
Student B: Because I was visiting the zoo.
Student A: Good. Your turn.
Student B: Why were you … ?

## Living English

# DUMB CRIMINALS

**Some criminals aren't very intelligent. Here are some funny stories!**

**A**

A burglar was stealing a laptop computer from a house. He left his cell phone on the table. The police found the phone, and called the burglar's house. They told him to pick up his cell phone at the police station. The burglar arrived at the police station and the police arrested him.

**B**

A man was traveling on a freeway in Colorado, in a special fast lane. It was only for cars with two or more passengers. A police officer was driving next to the man. The police officer saw that the passenger in the car wasn't moving. In fact, the passenger wasn't real. The man was riding with a dummy! The police fined him $115.

**C**

Two men stole a car from a gas station. The owner of the car was working in the station, and she called the police. An hour later she was cleaning the parking lot, when a car stopped at the station. It was her car! The thieves needed gas, so they came back to fill up! What were they thinking?

**D**

A man and a woman were robbing a convenience store. When the man was collecting the money, the woman saw a poster for a contest to win a car. She filled out a form with her name, address, and phone number. A few hours later, the police arrested the couple at the woman's house.

## Reading

**1** **Look at the Reading skills box.**

> **Reading skills**
>
> Using pictures and titles
> - **Look at the pictures and headings when you read. They can give you information about the main ideas.**

**2** **Look at the pictures, and read the title of the article. What is the article about?**

a stupid police officers
b stupid criminals

**3** **Read the article. What were the criminals doing? Write the letter of the story.**

1 robbing a store D
2 stealing from a home ........
3 breaking a traffic law ........
4 stealing a car ........

**4** **Choose the correct answer.**

1 The burglar in A lost his … .
a laptop (b) cell phone c house

2 … sitting in the car in B when the police stopped the car.
a One person was b Two people were
c Three people were

3 The car thieves in C returned because they wanted to … .
a return a car b win a car c get gas

4 The police in D had … .
a the woman's money b the woman's address
c the woman's cell phone

 → Workbook p.W24

# Listening

## Describing what you were doing

**1** Listen to the conversation. Who is the boy in the picture? Who is Michael?

**2** Listen to the conversation again. What was everyone doing at seven o'clock? Match the sentence halves.

1 Jay was — a shouting at Michael.
2 Hannah was — b shopping with Hannah.
3 Monica was — c shopping for clothes.
4 Michael was — d doing his homework.
5 Suzy was — e leaving the movie theater.

**3** Listen again. Circle the correct answer.

1 Last night, Michael was with … .
a Hannah b Jay c Suzy
2 Monica bought a new … .
a cell phone b jacket c book
3 Michael and Suzy were … .
a arguing b eating c fighting
4 Hannah says Michael was … .
a excited b happy c unhappy

# Speaking

## Expressing surprise

**1** Listen and read.

Gabby: What were you doing yesterday afternoon at two o'clock?
Jordan: I was running a marathon. I won first prize!
Gabby: No way! Is that true?
Jordan: No! I was cooking dinner!

Jordan: What were you doing at eight o'clock last night?
Gabby: I was recording a song for my album.
Jordan: You're kidding!
Gabby: Yes, I am. I was reading a book!

**2** Look at the Pronunciation box. Listen to the examples. Then listen again and repeat.

**Pronunciation**

/ʊ/ and /u/ sounds

| /ʊ/ | /u/ |
|---|---|
| good | do |
| book | you |
| cooking | afternoon |
| took | true |

**3** Listen. Check (✓) if the pronunciation is correct. Put an X (✗) if it is wrong.

1 do ✓
2 book
3 took
4 true
5 cooking
6 you
7 afternoon
8 good

**4** Practice the dialogue in exercise 1.

**5** Now change the words in blue. Write a new dialogue. Then practice the dialogue in class.

# Round-up

## Writing

### Telling a story

**1** **Read Carla's story.**

Last night, my friend Lydia and I were watching a DVD in my room. Suddenly, ~~Lydia and I~~ *we* heard a loud noise. It was coming from the yard. We saw a man, and Lydia thought it was a burglar! Lydia screamed, and I called the police. We were scared. It was very dark. The man was looking for something. The man was still there when the police arrived. When we saw his face, we realized it was my dad! My dad was looking for his keys. Lydia and I were laughing, but the police weren't laughing. The police were angry!

**2** **Look at the Writing skills box.**

**Writing skills**

Avoiding repetition

- **Don't repeat names and nouns a lot. You can use pronouns when it is clear what you mean.**
  Suddenly we heard a loud noise.
  ~~The loud noise~~ It was coming from the yard.

**3** **Look for repeated names and nouns in the story. Replace them with pronouns.**

**4** **Complete the chart with the information from Carla's story.**

| Carla's story | |
|---|---|
| Who were the people? | *Carla, Lydia* |
| What were they doing? | |
| What happened? | |
| What was the result? | |

**5** **Make a chart with notes for your own story.**

**6** **Write your story. Remember to use pronouns.**

## I can ...

**1** **Write sentences about yesterday evening. Use the past progressive.**

1 *I wasn't eating dinner at 8 p.m.*
2 ______________.
3 ______________.
4 ______________.

**I can describe what was happening at a specific time in the past.**

Yes, I can. ☐ I need more practice. ☐

**2** **Unscramble the words to make questions.**

1 with / Why / you / Emily / arguing / were
*Why were you arguing with Emily*?
2 doing / at / What / 10 p.m. / you / were
______________?
3 they / going / Where / yesterday / were
______________?
4 he / bus stop / When / was / at / the / waiting
______________?

**I can ask questions about activities in the past.**

Yes, I can. ☐ I need more practice. ☐

# 4 Disaster!

## Introducing the topic

## Vocabulary

### Natural disasters

**1** **Label the photos with the words below. Then listen, check, and repeat.**

blizzard drought ~~earthquake~~ flood
forest fire hurricane tornado tsunami

**2** **Listen to four reporters. What natural disasters are they talking about?**

1 flood
2 ____
3 ____
4 ____

**3** **Fill in the blanks with words from exercise 1.**

1 A serious drought can last for many years.
2 A ____ is a very big storm with strong winds.
3 A big ____ can burn down thousands of trees.
4 A lot of snow fell during the ____ .
5 A ____ is a very big wave.

**4** **Where do natural disasters sometimes happen? Write five sentences.**

Earthquakes sometimes happen in Chile.

## Exploring the topic

# 2012

At the start of the movie in 2009, people around the world were living their normal lives, but unusual things were happening. Scientist Adrian Helmsly was working in India when he discovered that the Earth's temperature was increasing very fast! Adrian predicted many natural disasters for the year 2012.

In 2010, scientists were working on a secret project to save everyone on Earth. They were building big boats called arks in the Himalayas. Secret agents were collecting paintings and books to save from the disasters.

In 2012, Jackson Curtis was camping with his family when the disasters started happening. Volcanoes were erupting and an earthquake destroyed Los Angeles. A tsunami hit Washington, D.C. and caused terrible floods. Then Jackson learned about the secret arks and decided to save his family.

He took his family to Las Vegas. Then they flew by airplane to the Himalayas, but there was an accident. Their airplane was landing when it crashed in the mountains. A giant tsunami was coming, but Jackson and his family got into one of the arks. At the end of the movie, some dry land was starting to appear, and there was hope for the survivors.

## Reading

**1** Read and listen to the article. Check (✓) which natural disasters are in the movie.

| | | | |
|---|---|---|---|
| drought | ☐ | forest fire | ☐ |
| tsunami | ☐ | flood | ☐ |
| earthquake | ☐ | | |

**2** Read again. Put the sentences in order.

a The Curtis family flew to Asia. ____
b Scientists were building ships called arks. ____
c Adrian Helmlsey was working in India. 1
d Some dry land started appearing again. ____
e An earthquake destroyed Los Angeles. ____
f The Curtis family was camping. ____
g Adrian discovered a serious problem. ____

**3** Answer the questions. Use full sentences.

1 What problem did Adrian discover in India?
*He discovered that the Earth's temperature was increasing very fast*.

2 What did secret agents save from the disasters?
____.

3 Where were the scientists building the arks?
____.

4 What was there in Washington, D.C.?
____.

5 Where did the Curtis family's airplane crash?
____.

# Grammar

## Past progressive and simple past

Talking about actions in progress and completed actions in the past

**1** **Look at the chart.**

| Past progressive | Simple past |
|---|---|
| I **was walking** home. | I **saw** my friend David. |
| You **were camping**. | It **started** to rain. |
| He **wasn't studying**. | His father **came** home. |
| They **weren't listening**. | The teacher **asked** a question. |

**2** **Match the actions in progress with the completed actions.**

1 Helen was swimming.
2 Jeff was skateboarding.
3 Lisa and Bea were sleeping.
4 Julia was cleaning her room.
5 Carlos was making breakfast.
6 Ted and Rina were hiking.

a He dropped an egg.
b They heard a noise.
c She saw a big fish.
d They got lost.
e He broke his leg.
f She found ten dollars.

**3** **Look at the chart.**

| Past progressive + *when* + simple past | | |
|---|---|---|
| He was working in India | **when** | he discovered something. |
| They were camping | | the disasters started. |
| Their airplane was landing | | it crashed in the mountains. |

**4** **Complete the sentences with *when* and the verbs in parentheses. Use the simple past.**

1 It was raining when we got (we / get) off the train.
2 I wasn't studying ______ (you / call) me last night.
3 We were having a picnic ______ (it / start) to rain.
4 They weren't sleeping ______ (the earthquake / happen).
5 He was riding his bike ______ (we / see) him in the park.
6 We were reading ______ (the door / open) suddenly.

**5** **Fill in the blanks. Use the past progressive first, and then the past simple.**

1 Daniel was running (run) when he lost (lose) his cell phone.
2 Maya ______ (drive) when she ______ (have) an accident.
3 We ______ (play) soccer when Mike ______ (fall) down.
4 My friends ______ (wait) for me when I ______ (arrive).
5 I ______ (cook) dinner when Suzy ______ (call).
6 You ______ (talk) with your friends when we ______ (see) you.

**Puzzle** page 85, puzzle 4A

**6** **Over to you!**

**Tell your friend about a good / bad dream. What was happening at first? Then what happened?**

Student A: What was happening in your dream?
Student B: I was surfing in Hawaii.
Student A: Then what happened?
Student B: A big wave hit me, and I fell.

# Building the topic

A Mark was sitting near Lynsey. He (1) politely asked the two boys to leave her alone.

B Lynsey jumped up and kicked the boy in the leg. She kicked him really (2) ________ !

C Lynsey was sitting (3) ________ on the bus. Two boys were annoying people in the back.

D Lynsey stayed cool and reacted very (4) ________ . Later, she got a medal for her bravery!

E The boys shouted (5) ________ at Mark. Then one of them attacked Mark with a knife.

F Mark was hurt (6) ________ , so the bus driver drove (7) ________ to the hospital.

G Lynsey looked back. The boys saw Lynsey and they walked towards her (8) ________ .

## Vocabulary

### Adverbs of manner

**1** **Read the texts quickly. Fill in the blanks with the adverbs of manner below. Then listen, check, and repeat.**

angrily badly carefully happily hard loudly ~~politely~~ well

**2** **Read the texts again. Match them with the pictures. Then listen and check.**

1 C
2 ____
3 ____
4 ____
5 ____
6 ____
7 ____

**3** **Circle the correct word.**

1 The girls smiled **happily** / **loudly** for the camera.
2 "Thank you very much," Alan said **badly** / **politely**.
3 Maggie sings very **hard** / **badly**. She's terrible!
4 I put the eggs in the refrigerator very **carefully** / **happily**.
5 We did **loudly** / **well** on the test because we studied a lot.
6 "Kick the ball **hard** / **badly**!" the boys shouted.

# Grammar

## Adverbs of manner

Talking about how we do things

**1 Look at the chart.**

| Regular adverbs | | |
|---|---|---|
| **Adjective** | **Adverb** | **Example** |
| loud | **loudly** | They were talking **loudly**. |
| happy | **happily** | She was smiling **happily**. |
| careful | **carefully** | He drove **carefully**. |
| **Irregular** | | |
| good | **well** | They reacted very **well**. |
| hard | **hard** | She kicked him **hard**. |
| fast | **fast** | I jumped up **fast**. |

**2 Fill in the blanks. Change the adjectives to adverbs.**

1 Jack is a careful driver. He's driving *carefully*.

2 Mary is a happy teacher. She teaches ______.

3 Seth is a good climber. He climbs ______.

4 Lionel is a fast driver. He drives ______.

5 The twins are angry. They're talking ______.

6 Sergio is a hard worker. He works ______.

**3 Fill in the blanks with the correct form of the words below.**

angry bad fast good ~~hard~~ loud

1 Aaron kicked the ball *hard*.

2 Val was singing ______.

3 Alice was running ______.

4 Pete was playing ______.

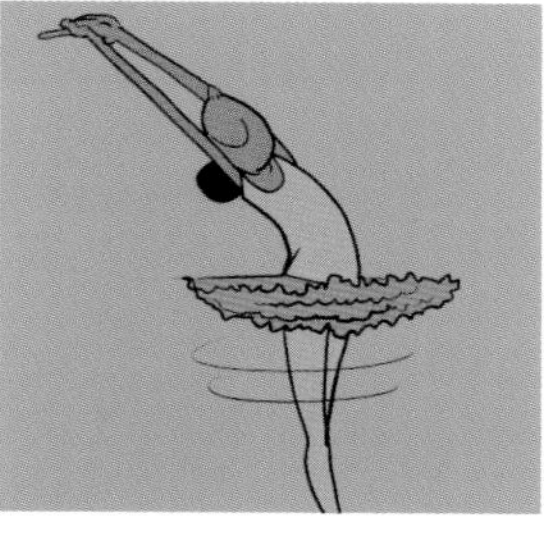

5 Lucy was dancing ______.

6 They were shouting ______.

**Take note!**

- **We use adjectives with nouns.**
  Bob is a quiet boy.
- **We use adverbs with verbs.**
  He opened the door quietly.

**4 Circle the correct adjective or adverb.**

I walked (1) slow / (slowly) to the bus stop. It was a (2) **beautiful / beautifully** day. At the bus stop, I met a (3) **happy / happily** girl. She talked (4) **polite / politely** to me. She was a (5) **famous / famously** climber from Austria. She talked (6) **slow / slowly** because her English wasn't very (7) **good / well**. The bus came, but it didn't stop, so we waited (8) **patient / patiently** for the next one.

**Puzzle** page 85, puzzle 4B

**5 Over to you!**

**Write five sentences about you. Use adverbs of manner. Then share them with a classmate.**

Student A: I play tennis well. And you?
Student B: Yes. I play tennis well.
Student A: OK. It's your turn.
Student B: I talk loudly. And you?
Student A: No. I don't talk loudly.

# A Story of Survival

In 1985, Joe Simpson and Simon Yates decided to climb Siula Grande, a tall mountain in Peru. After three days, they reached the top, but they didn't have much food left, and they needed to climb down quickly.

They were climbing down the mountain when something terrible happened. Simpson fell and broke his leg. The two men tied themselves together with a long rope and continued climbing down the mountain very slowly. But that wasn't the end of their problems. During a blizzard, Simpson fell off the edge of the mountain. Simpson was hanging from the rope when Yates started to fall, too.

Yates held the rope for an hour, and then he had to make a very difficult decision. He didn't want to die, and he thought his friend was dead. Yates decided to cut the rope, and then he continued down the mountain.

However, Simpson wasn't dead. He fell about 30 meters into an ice cave. It was cold and dark, and he didn't have any food or water, but he desperately wanted to live. He crawled out of the cave, and slowly began to crawl down the mountain. Three days later, Simpson arrived at the camp. Simon Yates also survived the blizzard. Later, Simpson wrote a book called *Touching the Void*. Hollywood also made a movie about this incredible story of survival.

## Reading

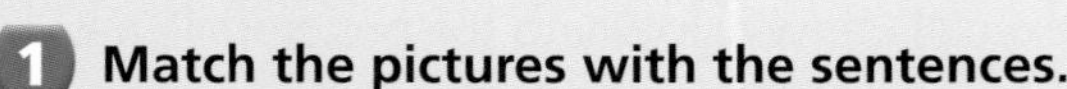

**1 Match the pictures with the sentences.**

1 He was holding the rope. A
2 He crawled down the mountain. ____
3 He decided to cut the rope. ____
4 He was hanging in the air. ____

**2 Read the story. Put the events in order.**

1 Simpson fell and broke his leg. ____
2 Yates and Simpson climbed Siula Grande. 1
3 There was a terrible blizzard. ____
4 Both climbers survived. ____
5 Yates and Simpson tied themselves together with a rope. ____

**3 Look at the Reading skills box.**

**Reading skills**

Summarizing a text

- **After you read a text, you can make a short summary. This helps you remember the most important parts.**

**4 Complete the summary with the words below.**

blizzard book cave ~~climbed~~ cut leg rope survived

**Climbers survive blizzard**

Simon Yates and Joe Simpson (1) climbed Siula Grande, in Peru. They were coming down the mountain when Simpson fell and broke his (2) ____. Simpson and Yates used a (3) ____ to go down. Later, there was a big (4) ____. Yates had to (5) ____ the rope, and Simpson fell into a (6) ____. In the end, both men (7) ____, and later, Simpson wrote a (8) ____.


Workbook p.W30

## Listening

### Apologizing

**1** **Look at the Listening skills box.**

> **Listening skills**
>
> Previewing the questions
>
> - **Before you listen, read the questions first. This helps you to understand better. It also helps you to hear the answers.**

**2** **Look at the questions for exercise 3. What do you think Gwen and Maria are talking about? Listen and check.**

a a movie on TV
b a vacation
c Gwen's new cell phone

**3** **Listen again. Circle the correct answer.**

1 Yesterday, Maria was … .
  a waiting for Gwen
  b eating a pizza
  c watching TV

2 At the same time, Gwen was … .
  a calling Maria
  b watching a movie
  c doing her homework

3 The tourists were … .
  a skiing
  b visiting a park
  c camping

4 The movie was about … .
  a a blizzard
  b a tornado
  c an earthquake

5 Finally, Gwen and Maria decide to … .
  a have lunch
  b go shopping
  c meet at the park

## Speaking

### Giving excuses

**1** **Listen and read.**

Mariella: I was waiting for you at the sports center this afternoon.
Jordan: I'm sorry. I feel terrible!
Mariella: What happened?
Jordan: I was reading my book when I fell asleep!

Chester: You're late.
Gabby: I know. I'm really sorry.
Chester: What happened?
Gabby: I was walking to the bus stop when I saw my friends.

**2** **Look at the Pronunciation box. Listen to the examples. Then listen again and repeat.**

> **Pronunciation**
>
> /i/ and /ɪ/ sounds

| /i/ | /ɪ/ |
|---|---|
| feel | this |
| reading | didn't |
| meet | missed |

**3** **Listen. Circle the word you hear.**

1 seat / sit
2 feel / fill
3 heat / hit
4 team / Tim
5 sheep / ship

**4** **Practice the dialogues in exercise 1.**

**5** **Now change the words in blue. Write new dialogues. Then practice the dialogues in class.**

# Round-up

## Writing

### A movie summary

**1** **Look at the Writing skills box.**

**Writing skills**

Narrative linkers

- **You can use narrative linkers when you are telling a story.**
  At first, everything was fine. Then, it started raining. Next, there was a hurricane. After that, there were floods. In the end, everyone was safe.

**2** **Read the movie summary. Put the main events in order.**

**WAR OF THE WORLDS**

Ray Ferrier was living in New Jersey. He was spending the weekend with his children, Robbie and Rachel, when something incredible happened.

☐ In the end, the aliens didn't win. They all became sick and died.

☐ Then, some alien ships came out of the ground. They started attacking people.

1 At first, there was a strange storm. Cars and other machines stopped working.

☐ After that, Ray caused a big explosion and destroyed the alien ship.

☐ Next, the Ferriers tried to escape to Boston, but an alien ship stopped them.

I liked this movie because it was exciting, and the ending was surprising. The special effects were great.

**3** **Complete in the chart with information about *War of the Worlds*.**

| Movie | *War of the Worlds* |
|---|---|
| The main characters | father: Ray<br>daughter:<br>son: |
| The beginning of the movie | |
| The main events | At first,<br>Then,<br>Next,<br>After that, |
| The end of the movie | In the end, |

**4** **Choose a disaster movie you like, or invent a new disaster movie. Make a chart with the information about your movie.**

**5** **Write a summary for your movie. Use your chart and the summary in exercise 2 to help you. Use narrative linkers.**

## I can ...

**1** **Complete the sentences with the simple past or past progressive.**

1 Maria was taking (take) a shower when we called (call).
2 We ________ (talk) about you when you ________ (arrive).
3 They ________ (sleep) when the alarm clock ________ (ring).

I can describe actions in progress and completed actions in the past.
Yes, I can. ☐ I need more practice. ☐

**2** **Circle the correct word.**

1 This is a very (quiet) / quietly city.
2 Fernando speaks English good / well.
3 He drove very careful / carefully.
4 The children are happy / happily.

I can describe how we do things.
Yes, I can. ☐ I need more practice. ☐

# B Review

## Vocabulary

### Conflict verbs

**1 Fill in the blanks with the correct form of the words below.**

argue complain ~~fight~~ hide hit shout

1 Wei and his brother never agree. They *fight* violently about everything.
2 Our cat always ............ under the bed.
3 We often ............ about the food at school. It isn't very good.
4 Don't ............ with me. I'm always right.
5 Don't ............ your brother. It isn't nice.
6 Please don't ............ . I can hear you.

### Places in a street

**2 Match the sentences with the places.**

1 "There's the bus stop." — f
2 "The building is on fire!"
3 "Where is your car parked?"
4 "You're under arrest."
5 "I need to get some money."
6 "I live on the fifth floor."

a bank
b apartment
c police station
d fire escape
e garage
f street corner

### Natural disasters

**3 Unscramble the words below.**

1 d a n o r o t *tornado*
2 z a b d r l i z ............
3 u a r h e c i n r ............
4 r o t s e f r e i f ............
5 m n s u i a t ............
6 o l o f d ............
7 k t r a e u a h q e ............
8 u r t g d o h ............

### Adverbs of manner

**4 Fill in the blanks with the adverb form of the words below.**

angry careful good ~~hard~~ polite

1 I get good grades because I work *hard* .
2 Our mom shouted at us ............ because we were fighting.
3 Our team usually wins. They play very ............ .
4 Kevin was walking ............ across the old bridge.
5 Please speak ............ to your teachers.

## Grammar

### Past progressive (affirmative / negative)

**1 Look at the picture. Write affirmative or negative sentences about Tanya and Josh in the past progressive.**

1 *They weren't running* .
(they / run)

2 ............ .
(Josh / look at a map)

3 ............ .
(Tanya / drive)

4 ............ .
(Josh / take a photo)

5 ............ .
(Tanya / shout)

6 ............ .
(they / laugh)

## B Review

### Past progressive (questions)

**2 Write questions for Tanya's answers.**

Ali: (1) What were you doing at eleven o'clock yesterday?
Tanya: I was driving at eleven o'clock yesterday.
Ali: (2) ____________?
Tanya: I was going to Detroit.
Ali: (3) ____________?
Tanya: I was going there because I wanted to visit my parents.
Ali: (4) ____________?
Tanya: Josh was with me.
Ali: (5) ____________?
Tanya: We were arguing.
Ali: (6) ____________?
Tanya: We were arguing because we were lost!

### Past progressive and simple past

**3 Fill in the blanks with the past progressive form of the verbs in parentheses.**

I (1) was walking (walk) along the beach with a friend. The sun (2) ____________ (shine), and some beautiful birds (3) ____________ (sing). Some people (4) ____________ (play) beach volleyball, and two older people (5) ____________ (read) newspapers. A teenage girl (6) ____________ (listen) to music.

**4 Finish the story. Fill in the blanks with the simple past form of the verbs in parentheses.**

Then a strong wind (1) hit (hit) the coast and it (2) ____________ (start) to rain. The birds (3) ____________ (fly) away, and the people (4) ____________ (run) to their cars and (5) ____________ (drive) home. We (6) ____________ (go) to a café and (7) ____________ (wait) for the storm to end.

### Adverbs of manner

**5 Fill in the blanks with the adverb form of the words in parentheses.**

1 I shouted loudly (loud), but my mom didn't hear me.
2 Brad smiled ____________ (happy). He passed the test.
3 My dad always drives very ____________ (careful).
4 They climbed the mountain ____________ (easy).
5 Our team played ____________ (good), but they lost.
6 It was raining ____________ (hard) when we arrived.

### Study skills

**English outside the classroom**

**1 Match the words below with the pictures of places you can see or hear English.**

| 3 advertisements | movies | signs |
|---|---|---|
| song lyrics | restaurants | |

**2 Try to find ten English words outside the classroom and write them in your notebook.**


MultiROM

# 5 What's your style?

## Introducing the topic

## Vocabulary

### Hair and clothes

**1** Look at the picture and fill in the blanks in the profiles with the words below. Then listen, check, and repeat.

baggy curly high long low ~~short~~ straight tall tight wavy

**1 Kuan**
height: (1) *short*
hair: short and (2) ..........
shirt: big and baggy
pants: long and (3) ..........
shoes: low heels

**2 Areesha**
height: short
hair: short and (4) ..........
T-shirt: baggy
skirt: (5) ..........
boots: (6) .......... heels

**3 Belinda**
height: (7) ..........
hair: long and (8) ..........
jacket: short
jeans: long and (9) ..........
boots: (10) .......... heels

**2** Complete the chart with the words in exercise 1. You can use some words twice.

| | |
|---|---|
| **For hair** | *short;* |
| **For clothes** | *baggy;* |

**3** How do you look today? Fill in your information below.

1 Your hair: .......... and ..........
2 Your pants / jeans / skirt: ..........
3 Your shirt / T-shirt / jacket: ..........
4 Your shoes / boots: ..........

Workbook p.W32 → MultiROM

## Exploring the topic

# BEST FRIENDS, DIFFERENT STYLES

1

Sasha and Kate are best friends, but they have very different styles. Take a look at their photos!

Sasha's hair is longer than Kate's hair, but it isn't as straight as Kate's. Sasha isn't taller than her best friend, but she's wearing shoes with higher heels in this photo, and that makes a big difference. Sasha's pants are tighter than Kate's. "Baggy pants are very comfortable, but I think tight jeans look better," Sasha says.

Kate's hair is shorter than Sasha's. In this photo, she has her hair in a ponytail. Kate is wearing a tighter T-shirt than Sasha, but Kate's pants are baggier. Kate is also wearing lower shoes. "I like being comfortable, especially when I'm shopping," she says. "I don't worry a lot about fashion."

What do the girls say about their personal styles? Sasha says, "We look different and dress differently, but that isn't important." Kate says, "We're best friends, but we aren't identical, and you can see that in our style."

2

## Reading

**1 Read and listen to the article. Match the photos with the names.**

Photo 1: ............ Photo 2: ............

**2 Read again. Then read the sentences and write *Sasha* or *Kate*.**

1 She's wearing higher shoes than her friend. Sasha
2 Her hair is longer than her friend's hair. ............
3 She likes wearing bigger, baggier jeans. ............
4 Her shoes are lower than her friend's shoes. ............
5 She doesn't think about fashion very much. ............
6 Her T-shirt is tighter than her friend's T-shirt. ............

**3 Answer the questions.**

1 Why does Sasha like tight jeans?
she thinks they look better
2 Who is wearing sportier clothes?
............
3 Why does Kate wear lower shoes?
............
4 Who prefers baggy clothes?
............
5 Why does Sasha look taller than Kate?
............

# Grammar

## Short comparative adjectives

Talking about differences

**1** **Look at the chart.**

| Comparative adjective + *than* + noun |
|---|
| Sasha's hair is dark**er than** Kate's hair. |
| Kate's hair isn't long**er than** Sasha's hair. |
| Kate's pants are bagg**ier than** Sasha's jeans. |
| Sasha's shoes aren't low**er than** Kate's shoes. |

### Take note!

**Spelling rules for short comparative adjectives**

- **add *-er* or *-r***
  long ➜ longer
  nice ➜ nicer
- **consonant + ~~y~~ + *-ier***
  curly ➜ curlier
  wavy ➜ wavier
- **double consonant + *-er***
  big ➜ bigger
  thin ➜ thinner

**Irregular**
good ➜ better
bad ➜ worse

**2** **Fill in the blanks with the comparative form of the adjectives in parentheses.**

1 This jacket is *baggier* than my jacket. (baggy)
2 Our cat is ............ than your cat. (fat)
3 This book is ............ than that book. (funny)
4 Dan's hair is ............ than my hair. (short)
5 Motorcycles are ............ than bikes. (noisy)
6 Our car is ............ than your car. (good)

**3** **Look at the charts and fill in the blanks below.**

| | David | Jerry |
|---|---|---|
| 1 | 1.80 m | 1.85 m |
| 2 | thin | very thin |
| 3 | curly hair | straight hair |
| 4 | good singer | bad singer |
| 5 | baggy clothes | tight clothes |
| 6 | good student | excellent student |

1 Jerry is *taller than* David.
2 Jerry is ............ David.
3 David has ............ hair ............ Jerry.
4 Jerry is a ............ singer ............ David.
5 David wears ............ clothes ............ Jerry.
6 Jerry is a ............ student ............ David.

**4** **Look at the picture. Write complete sentences.**

1 tree / tall / house
*The tree is taller than the house*.
2 truck / big / car ............
3 cat / clean / dog ............
4 motorcycle / fast / bus ............
5 girl / tall / boy ............
6 girl's hair / curly / boy's hair ............

**Puzzle** page 87, puzzle 5A

**5** **Over to you!**

**Compare yourself to friends or people in your family. Use the comparative form of short adjectives in your sentences.**
Student A: I'm taller than my best friend.
Student B: I'm better at English than my brother.

## Building the topic

My brother Caleb is very (1) *sociable* . He loves being with people. My friend Katia is more (2) ________ than my other friends. When I have a problem, she always helps me.
**Laura, Sydney, Australia**

My friend Niklas is more (3) ________ than me. His room is a disaster! My sister Elke is very (4) ________ . She paints, writes stories, and plays the guitar.
**Dieter, Berlin, Germany**

My best friend Luisa is as (5) ________ as I am. When we play sports, we both want to win! Her brother Diego is really (6) ________ . He never stops talking!
**Adam, Curitiba, Brazil**

My friend Jao is very (7) ________ . He's always smiling and happy! Jao isn't as (8) ________ as my best friend Sarai. She always cries when we watch sad movies!
**Nataya, Bangkok, Thailand**

## Vocabulary

### Personality adjectives

**1** **Look at the photos. Fill in the blanks with the words below. Then listen, check, and repeat.**

cheerful competitive creative disorganized helpful sensitive ~~sociable~~ talkative

**2** **Listen to eight people. Which adjective in exercise 1 describes each person?**

1 She's *disorganized* .
2 He's ________ .
3 She's ________ .
4 He's ________ .
5 She's ________ .
6 He's ________ .
7 She's ________ .
8 He's ________ .

**3** **Write five sentences to describe people you know. Use the adjectives in exercise 1.**

*My friend Alicia is really competitive.*

# Grammar

## Long comparative adjectives

Talking about differences

**1 Look at the chart.**

| ***more* + adjective + *than*** |
|---|
| Luisa is **more** competitive **than** me. |
| Dieter is **more** creative **than** his sister. |

**2 Fill in the blanks with the comparative form of the adjectives in parentheses.**

1 Jason is *more cheerful than* Robert. (cheerful)
2 Books are ............ DVDs. (interesting)
3 London is ............ Dublin. (expensive)
4 Skateboards are ............ bikes. (dangerous)
5 The train is ............ the bus. (comfortable)
6 Watching TV is ............ playing sports. (boring)

**3 Write comparative sentences.**

1 Climbing / difficult / cycling
*Climbing is more difficult than cycling*.
2 Kyle / talkative / his sister
............
3 Al / sensitive / Vladimir
............
4 My story / exciting / your story
............
5 Your clothes / colorful / my clothes
............

## (*not*) *as* ... *as*

Talking about similarities and differences

**4 Look at the chart.**

| **(*not*) *as* + adjective + *as*** |
|---|
| I'm **as** tall **as** Tom. We're the same height. |
| Liu is **not as** cheerful **as** Kelly. Kelly is more cheerful. |

**5 Fill in the blanks with (*not*) *as* ... *as*, and the adjectives in parentheses.**

1 I'm *not as tall as* John. He's 1.65 m and I'm 1.60 m tall. (tall)
2 Girls are ............ boys. There's no difference. (creative)
3 You are ............ Tom. He tells better jokes. (funny)
4 The weather today is ............ it was yesterday. It's warmer today. (cold)
5 Ahn is ............ I am. We both get good grades. (intelligent)

**6 Look at the chart. Write sentences comparing the two activities.**

| | skiing | running |
|---|---|---|
| 1 difficult | ★★★ | ★ |
| 2 tiring | ★★ | ★★ |
| 3 exciting | ★★★ | ★ |
| 4 cheap | ★ | ★★ |
| 5 popular | ★★★ | ★★★ |

1 Running *isn't as difficult as* skiing.
2 Skiing ............ running.
3 Running ............ skiing.
4 Skiing ............ running.
5 Running ............ skiing.

Puzzle page 87, puzzle 5B

**7 Over to you!**

**Say two activities. Make a correct sentence to compare them.**
Student A: Swimming and scuba diving.
Student B: Scuba diving is more dangerous than swimming.

Workbook p.W35

Living English

# SERIOUS STYLING

1

2

3

4

5

### HIP-HOP

Pants for boys and girls are big and baggy. Boys' T-shirts are big, too, but girls' tops are smaller and tighter. Hip-hop style is modern, but it has a long history. It began in the 1920s with jazz music. Men often wore big, baggy suits called *zoot suits*!

### GRUNGE

The grunge style started with grunge music in the U.S. It's a lot more comfortable than other styles because the clothes are casual – just jeans and shirts, in plain colors. They're cheaper, too! Just don't wear anything very new – or very clean!

### PUNK

The punk style comes from punk music in the 1970s. It isn't as easy or as comfortable as other styles. It's really hard work! Punks have to color and style their hair often. Their clothes are also tighter than other styles, and usually black. Make-up is also really important for punks.

### JAPANESE STREET

This style is more creative than others because everybody looks different – and strange! The idea is to wear more unusual clothes than anyone else. You also want crazier make-up and a more bizarre hairstyle. Some people also like to dress like action heroes and fantasy characters.

### HIPPIE

This style is from the late 1960s, but it comes back again and again. The hippie style expresses ideas of nature, peace, and freedom. It is also more artistic than many other styles. Hippie clothes are colorful, and they often have flowers and other patterns on them.

## Reading

**1 Look at the pictures. What do you call these styles in your language? What are the main characteristics of the styles?**

**2 Read the article. Match the pictures with the styles.**

grunge ____ hip-hop 1 Japanese street ____
hippie ____ punk ____

**3 Read the article again. Write the name of the style(s) next to the statements.**

1 These styles are related to kinds of music.
hip-hop ____ ____

2 This style is not easy to have.
____

3 This style started in the 1920s. ____

4 Bright colors are important in this style.
____

5 Make-up is important in these styles.
____ ____

6 New clothes are not a part of this style.
____

**4 Think about it**
**What kind of clothes do you like to wear? What's your style?**

 Workbook p.W36

## Listening
### Comparing clothes

**1** 🔊 **Listen to the conversation between Tina and Bob. Check (✓) the adjectives below that you hear.**

1 longer ✓
2 darker ☐
3 thinner ☐
4 baggier ☐
5 tighter ☐
6 colorful ☐

**2** 🔊 **Listen again. Circle the correct word.**

1 Amelia's hair is (shorter) / longer than Tina's.
2 Tina is **taller / shorter** than Amelia.
3 Amelia's jeans are **baggier / tighter** than Tina's.
4 Tina's clothes are **more / less** colorful than Amelia's clothes.
5 Amelia's bag is **bigger / smaller** than Tina's.

**3** **Look at the Listening skills box.**

**Listening skills**

Discussing your ideas

- **When you practice listening, you can compare your answers with a classmate.**

**Now circle the correct options. Compare your answers with a friend. Do you agree or disagree?**

1 Which people are going to a concert?
(a) Amelia and Tina.
b Tina and Bob.
c all three people.

2 Who has darker hair: Amelia or Tina?
a Tina's hair is darker.
b Amelia's hair is as dark as Tina's.
c Amelia's hair is darker.

3 Amelia's boyfriend is … .
a shorter than Bob
b older than Bob
c bigger than Bob

## Speaking
### At a clothes store

**1** 🔊 **Listen and read.**

Sales clerk: Can I help you?
Gabby: I'm looking for a new dress.
Sales clerk: How about this one?
Gabby: Do you have anything baggier?

Sales clerk: How about this dress?
Gabby: That looks nice. Can I try it on?
Sales clerk: Of course. The fitting rooms are over there.
Gabby: Thanks!

**2** 🔊 **Look at the Pronunciation box. Listen to the examples. Then listen again and repeat.**

**Pronunciation**

Linked sounds

- **We link some sounds in a sentence.**

Can‿I help you? I'm looking for‿a new dress.
How‿about this‿one? Can‿I try‿it‿on?

**3** 🔊 **Draw the linked sounds in the sentences. Then listen, check, and repeat.**

1 Are you doing‿your math‿homework?
2 He's wearing a pair of blue shoes.
3 When do you want to eat lunch?
4 I made a mistake in the exam.
5 They aren't at home right now.

**4** **Practice the dialogue in exercise 1.**

**5** **Now change the words in blue. Write a new dialogue. Then practice the dialogue in class.**

# Round-up

## Writing

### My favorite person

**1** Look at the Writing skills box.

**Writing skills**

Order of adjectives

- **Use the following order for two or more adjectives in the same sentence: size + age + color**
  He often wears a big, old, blue shirt.
- **We put a comma between adjectives in a list.**
  My dad has short, fair hair.

**2** Read the text about Carlos's favorite person. Who is his favorite person? Name three good qualities of his favorite person.

My brother Rafael is my favorite person. He is three years older than I am. He is shorter than me, but he is stronger. His hair is shorter than mine, and his clothes are more fashionable. He always looks really good.

I really like Rafael's personality. He is very sociable. He talks to new people all the time, and he loves going to parties with his friends. Rafael is more cheerful than other people, too. He is always laughing. And he is more helpful than anyone I know. He always does good things for people, and he always does them with a smile.

**3** Fill in the chart with information about Rafael. Give examples of his qualities.

| My favorite person | |
|---|---|
| Name / Relation | *Rafael, my brother* |
| Physical appearance | |
| Style | |
| Personality | |

**4** Make a chart with information about your favorite person. Use adjectives to describe their physical appearance, style, and personality.

**5** Write a description of your favorite person from exercise 4. Use Carlos's description and your chart to help you. Check the order of the adjectives.

## I can ...

**1** Write sentences comparing you and your family.

1 *My father is taller than me* .
2 ............ .
3 ............ .
4 ............ .

**I can compare people in my family.**
Yes, I can. ☐ I need more practice. ☐

**2** Complete the sentences with the correct comparative. Use the adjectives in parentheses.

1 Your sister is *as cheerful as* mine. (cheerful)
2 Cars are ............ planes. There are more car accidents. (dangerous)
3 London is not ............ Tokyo. Japan is very expensive. (expensive)

**I can describe similarities and differences.**
Yes, I can. ☐ I need more practice. ☐

# 6 Amazing places

## Introducing the topic

1 a modern museum

2 a ________ river

3 a ________ canyon

4 a ________ rainforest

5 a ________ statue

6 a ________ desert

7 a ________ subway

8 a ________ street

## Vocabulary

### Adjectives for places

**1** **Look at the photos. Fill in the blanks with the adjectives below. Then listen, check, and repeat.**

crowded deep dry large ~~modern~~ narrow wet wide

**2** **Circle the correct word.**

1 The Nile is a long, **wide** / **dry** river in Africa.
2 Taipei 101 is a **modern** / **deep** building in Taipei.
3 New York and Tokyo are very **narrow** / **crowded** cities.
4 The Smithsonian is a **large** / **wet** museum in Washington, D.C.
5 Antarctica is a very cold and **dry** / **modern** place.
6 The Grand Canyon is very long and **crowded** / **deep**.

**3** **Write five sentences about your city or country. Use adjectives from exercise 1.**

*There are a lot of modern buildings in my city.*

## Exploring the topic

# THAT'S A RECORD!
## READ AND BE AMAZED!

**1** The driest place in the world is the Atacama Desert in Chile. Usually it only rains every 100 years! If you visit, don't forget to take warm clothes. The temperature is between 0 and 25 degrees Celsius.

**2** Mauna Loa, on Hawaii, is the largest volcano on Earth. The volcano's name means "long mountain" in Hawaiian. Mauna Loa's last big eruption was in 1984.

**3** The wettest place in the world is Mawsynram, a village in India. It gets about 11.8 meters of rain per year! On July 1st, 1952, it rained almost one meter in 24 hours!

**4** Monaco, in Europe, is the most crowded country in the world, with about 17,000 people per square kilometer. Australia only has about three people per square kilometer!

**5** Lake Baikal in Siberia, Russia, is the deepest lake on Earth. It is 1,637 meters deep. Lake Baikal is also the oldest lake in the world. It's about 25 million years old!

**6** The Rio de la Plata is the widest river in the world. It's between Argentina and Uruguay. At the river's widest point, it's about 220 kilometers wide.

**7** Commonwealth Bay in Antarctica is the windiest place on Earth. The wind is sometimes faster than 200 kilometers per hour! That's amazing!

## Reading

**1** **Look at the pictures. Match them to four of the texts.** A 1 B ____ C ____ D ____

**2** **Read and listen to the article. Write the name of the correct place.**

1 It is a very wide river.
Rio de la Plata

2 It rains a lot every year here.
____

3 It's very dry.
____

4 It isn't a very crowded country.
____

5 It's very cold and very windy.
____

6 It has a volcano named "long mountain".
____

**3** **Answer the questions.**

1 How old is Lake Baikal?
25 million years old

2 What does "Mauna Loa" mean?
____

3 What is the temperature in the Atacama Desert?
____

4 Where is the Rio de la Plata?
____

5 How fast can the wind blow in Commonwealth Bay?
____
____

6 How much rain falls every year in Mawsynram?
____

# Grammar

## Superlative adjectives

Talking about special things

**1 Look at the chart.**

| *the* + superlative + noun |
|---|
| It's **the largest** volcano on Earth. |
| It's **the most crowded** country in the world. |

### Take note!

Spelling rules for superlative adjectives

**Short adjectives**

- **add *-est* or *-st***
  old ➜ the oldest
  large ➜ the largest
- **consonant + ~~y~~ + *-iest***
  windy ➜ the windiest
- **double consonant + *-est***
  wet ➜ the wettest

**Long adjectives**

boring ➜ the most boring
difficult ➜ the most difficult

**Irregular**

good ➜ the best
bad ➜ the worst

**2 Circle the correct form.**

1 Jake is (the shortest) / the most short boy in the class.
2 I think London is the interesting / the most interesting city in the world.
3 The Great Wall of China is the most biggest / the biggest man-made object in the world.
4 This restaurant has the worst / the baddest food in town.
5 Kara is the fastest / the fastiest runner on the team.

**3 Look at the pictures. Fill in the blanks with the superlative form of the adjectives below.**

crowded difficult good scary ~~tall~~ young

1 Andy is the tallest person in the class.

2 This is .................. .................. exercise in the test.

3 *Ghost Ship* is .................. movie in the world!

4 Dana is .................. .................. person in our family.

5 This is .................. .................. classroom in school.

6 When Paco won, it was .................. day of his life.

**4 Write superlative sentences.**

1 Joe's / good restaurant / in town
Joe's is the best restaurant in town.
2 Kelly / tall girl / in the team ..................
.................. .
3 my village / beautiful place / in the country
..................
.................. .
4 Jan's school / big / in the city ..................
.................. .
5 my MP3 player / expensive / in the store
..................
.................. .

Puzzle page 87, puzzle 6A

**5 Over to you!**

**Give opinions about people and places with superlative forms of adjectives.**

Student A: I think Kany García is the goodest singer in the world.
Student B: Sorry – that isn't a correct sentence.
Student A: I think Kany García is the best singer in the world.

## Building the topic

# Come to BEAUTIFUL BALI on vacation!

Home | Flights | Hotels | Travel tips | FAQs | Search:

1 2 3 4 5 6 7 8

## Travel tips for visitors

→ You should always carry your (1) *passport* in your bag.

→ Don't forget your (2) ............ ! You need it at the airport.

→ A digital (3) ............ is great because you can take a lot of photos.

→ You should take (4) ............ to tropical countries.

→ Remember to pack a (5) ............ for the beach!

→ Do you want to go for a nature walk? You should bring some (6) ............ .

→ Buy a good (7) ............ and read it before you leave home.

→ You shouldn't go out in the sun without (8) ............ !

## Vocabulary

### Travel items

**1** **Look at the pictures. Fill in the blanks in the travel tips with the words below. Then listen and check.**

camera e-ticket guidebook hiking boots insect spray ~~passport~~ sunblock swimsuit

**2** **Read the descriptions and write the words in exercise 1.**

1 People wear it in the water. *swimsuit*
2 It gives you information. ............
3 It protects you from the sun. ............
4 It has your photo and personal information. ............
5 You use it to keep mosquitoes away. ............
6 It tells you when your airplane leaves. ............
7 You use it to take photos. ............
8 They are comfortable to walk in on long journeys. ............

**3** **Think of a foreign country to visit. What things in exercise 1 should you pack?**

*Canada: I should pack insect spray, ...*

## Grammar

### *should / shouldn't*

Giving and asking for advice

**1** **Look at the chart.**

| Affirmative | Negative |
|---|---|
| You **should** use sunblock. | You **shouldn't** carry a lot of money. |
| **Questions** | **Answers** |
| **Should** I take a passport? | Yes, you **should**. No, you **shouldn't**. |
| What clothes **should** I take? | You **should** take pants and T-shirts. |

**2** **Look at the pictures. Circle *should* or *shouldn't*.**

1 You **should** / **shouldn't** drink the water.

2 He **should** / **shouldn't** use sunblock.

3 She **should** / **shouldn't** go outside today.

4 They **should** / **shouldn't** learn Chinese.

5 We **should** / **shouldn't** go in that taxi.

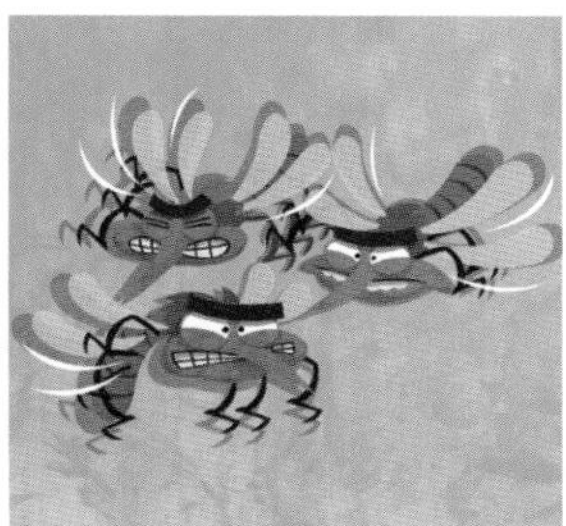

6 You **should** / **shouldn't** buy some insect spray.

**3** **Put the words in order to make sentences.**

1 sit / should / at a desk / You
You should sit at a desk .

2 should / take / You / regular breaks
................................................ .

3 study / shouldn't / You / for a long time
................................................ .

4 a good lamp / should / use / You
................................................ .

5 shouldn't / watch TV / You
................................................ .

6 lie down / You / shouldn't
................................................ .

**4** **Write questions with *should* and the words in parentheses.**

1 We hate hot weather. (When / we / go / to India?)
When should we go to India ?

2 I want to visit Ireland. (What / I / do / there?)
................................................ ?

3 Dan wants to learn to swim. (he / take / lessons?)
................................................ ?

4 They need to pass the test. (What / they / study?)
................................................ ?

5 She doesn't like pasta. (What / she / eat?)
................................................ ?

**5** **Match the answers with the questions in exercise 4.**

a You should go hiking. 2
b She should have some rice. ......
c Yes, he should. ......
d We should go in December. ......
e They should study word lists. ......

**Puzzle** page 87, puzzle 6B

**6** **Over to you!**

**Write suggestions for visitors to your country.**

Tourists should visit the capital city because it has a lot of museums.
They shouldn't come in August because the weather is too hot.

# YOUTH TRAVEL

My dad is in the army, so we visit a lot of different countries. For me, the coolest city for young people is definitely Glasgow, Scotland. Glasgow has the best music scene in the world, and it has the greatest museums and galleries, too. It's also one of the best cities for sports – especially soccer and rugby. What's the worst thing about Glasgow? It's pretty expensive, so you should take extra money, just in case! It can also be wet, so it's a good idea to take a jacket.

**Bryan, Memphis**

Gothenburg, Sweden, is definitely the best city in Europe. It's one of the coldest cities, too, so you should take warm clothes with you! Gothenburg is the most beautiful city in Sweden, and it's also Scandinavia's largest port. You don't need a lot of money in Gothenburg, and you can find a lot of cheap things to do. There is an exciting music scene in the city, too, so try to see a concert. You don't have to travel far from Gothenburg to enjoy nature, and winter sports are very popular.

**Annika, Stockholm**

My favorite place is Patong Beach in Phuket, Thailand. It's the best place in the world for young people. You can do everything there: go to great beaches, meet cool people, and go dancing. You should also try some typical food, like Thai noodles! The most crowded season of the year is the dry season, between December and March, so you should visit Phuket in October or April, when it's quieter.

**Mai, Bangkok**

## Reading

**1** **Look at the Reading skills box.**

> **Reading skills**
>
> Scanning quickly for information
>
> - **We sometimes scan a text quickly to find specific information. Then we can read the text again to understand all the details.**

**2** **Scan the articles, and write the letters of the paragraph(s) where you find the following words.**

1 money A B
2 dancing ____
3 winter ____
4 beaches ____
5 music ____ ____
6 museums ____

**3** **Choose the correct answer.**

1 Glasgow is great if … .
  (a) you have a lot of money
  b you are in the army
  c you like hot weather
  d you play the guitar

2 Gothenburg is … than Glasgow.
  a warmer
  b cheaper
  c more exciting
  d more popular

3 You should visit Gothenburg if you like … .
  a running
  b traveling
  c singing
  d skiing

4 Patong Beach is excellent if you … .
  a are beautiful
  b are cool
  c are quiet
  d are young

**4** **Think about it**

**What are the best and the worst things about your city?**


Workbook p.W42

## Listening

### At the travel agency

**1** Listen. Alice is at a travel agency. Circle the places you hear.

| | | | |
|---|---|---|---|
| Australia | Ireland | Scotland | Tokyo |
| Canada | London | Toronto | |

**2** Listen again. Circle T (True) or F (False).

1 Alice enjoys going to the beach. T / F
2 She doesn't like camping very much. T / F
3 Alice thinks big cities are interesting. T / F
4 She likes going to crowded places. T / F
5 Alice wants to go shopping. T / F

**3** Circle the correct answer.

1 When does Alice want to go on vacation?
a next week b next month
2 At the beach, Alice always feels … .
a bored b hot
3 She thinks camping isn't … enough.
a comfortable b exciting
4 Alice wants … vacation.
a an interesting b a relaxing
5 The travel agent says that Edinburgh is very … .
a historic b modern

## Speaking

### Giving advice

**1** Listen and read.

Mariella: Where should I go on vacation?
Gabby: I don't know. What do you want to do?
Mariella: I want to relax on a sunny beach!
Gabby: You should go to Brazil! It has some of the best beaches in the world!

Chester: I want to go camping this summer.
Jordan: You should go to Yosemite National Park, in California.
Chester: Are you sure? Is it a good place to go camping?
Jordan: Yes! I went there last year, and it was fantastic!

**2** Look at the Pronunciation box. Listen to the examples. Then listen again and repeat.

**Pronunciation**

/s/ and /ʃ/ sounds

| /s/ | /ʃ/ |
|---|---|
| sunny | should |
| summer | sure |
| fantastic | vacation |

**3** Listen to the sentences. Then complete the chart with the underlined words.

1 Sue dropped her shoe at the beach.
2 You should see the new show this weekend.
3 Sam shouldn't run so fast.

| /s/ | /ʃ/ |
|---|---|
| Sue; | |
| | |

**4** Practice the dialogues in exercise 1.

**5** Now change the words in blue. Write new dialogues. Then practice the dialogues in class.

# Round-up

## Writing

### A vacation brochure

**1** **Look at the Writing skills box.**

**Writing skills**

Checking your grammar and spelling

- **Check your spelling when you write up your work.**

  Oaxaca is ~~beautyfull~~ beautiful.

**2** **Read the brochure. Then correct the mistakes in red. Are they grammar mistakes (G) or spelling mistakes (Sp)?**

**3** **Complete the chart with information about Oaxaca.**

| Place | Oaxaca, Mexico |
|---|---|
| Best things | high mountains; |
| Weather | |
| Shopping | |
| Food and drink | |

**4** **Make a chart with information about a vacation place you know.**

**5** **Write a brochure about your vacation place. Use the brochure and your chart to help you. Find a photo of the place.**

## COME TO OAXACA!

G **Oaxaca is one of the ~~more~~ beautiful places in Mexico. It has high mountains, long beaches, and the friendlyest people! Here are some tips for visitors:** most

- **WEATHER**

  The weather in Oaxaca is wonderful. You shouldn't to take a lot of warm clothes because temperatures are always about 20° C.

- **SHOPPING**

  Oaxaca is a great place to shop, but don't buy everything in moden stores. You should go to the street market to get cheapest prices!

- **FOOD AND DRINK**

  Everyone should try some Oaxacan sausage. It's delicous! And don't forget to have some traditional hot chocolate! Tourists they shouldn't drink tap water in Oaxaca. They should always drink bottled water.

## I can ...

**1** **Complete the sentences with the superlative of the adjective in parentheses.**

1 The largest ______ volcano in the world is in Hawaii. (large)
2 Monaco is the ______ city in the world. (crowded)
3 Lake Baikal in Russia is the ______ lake on Earth. (deep)

I can describe special places.

Yes, I can. ☐ I need more practice. ☐

**2** **Match the sentence halves.**

1 It's raining hard. b
2 You have an English exam tomorrow. ___
3 That fish smells terrible! ___
4 I'm going to the U.S. next month. ___

a You shouldn't eat it.
b You should take your umbrella.
c Should I get a visa?
d You should start studying now.

I can ask for and give advice.

Yes, I can. ☐ I need more practice. ☐

# C Review

## Vocabulary

### Hair and clothes

**1** **Write the adjectives.**

1 straight hair
2 a .......... jacket
3 .......... jeans
4 .......... shoes
5 .......... hair
6 .......... hair
7 a .......... jacket
8 .......... jeans
9 .......... boots

### Personality adjectives

**2** **Fill in the blanks with the correct adjectives.**

1 I'm not very sensitive . I don't cry or get angry easily.
2 Kyra is very .......... . She's never quiet!
3 Ada is .......... . She designs clothes.
4 Paul isn't .......... at games. He doesn't care about winning.
5 Toni is .......... . Her room is very messy!
6 Sara's very .......... . She always helps me when I have a problem.
7 Juan loves being with people. He's very .......... .

### Adjectives for places

**3** **Fill in the blanks with adjectives for places.**

1 a crowded room

2 a .......... desert

3 a .......... river

4 a .......... house

5 a .......... valley

6 a .......... city

### Travel items

**4** **Read the descriptions and write the items.**

1 You use it to take photos. camera
2 It gives you information about a country. ..........
3 You wear it at the beach. ..........
4 It protects you on sunny days. ..........
5 You wear them for walking. ..........
6 Mosquitoes don't like it. ..........
7 You need this to go on an airplane. ..........
8 You can travel to other countries with it. ..........

Review

# Grammar

## Comparative adjectives

**1 Fill in the blanks with the comparative form of the underlined adjectives.**

1 Mike is tall, but Dave is taller .
2 Kim's dog is fat, but my dog is ______ .
3 Rob's bike is expensive, but Ted's is ______ .
4 Vicky's jeans are tight, but Cal's are ______ .
5 Lou's jeans are comfortable, but Ed's are ______ .
6 Sheila is happy, but Jon is ______ .

## (not) as … as

**2 Look at the chart about the two tours. Then fill in the blanks in the sentences with (*not*) *as* … *as* and the correct adjective.**

| | Tour A | Tour B |
|---|---|---|
| 1 long | ★ | ★ |
| 2 exciting | ★★★ | ★★ |
| 3 expensive | ★★★ | ★★★ |
| 4 dangerous | ★ | ★★ |
| 5 popular | ★★ | ★★ |

1 Tour A is as long as Tour B.
2 Tour B ______ Tour A.
3 Tour A ______ Tour B.
4 Tour A ______ Tour B.
5 Tour B ______ Tour A.

## Superlative adjectives

**3 Fill in the blanks with the superlative form of the adjectives in parentheses.**

1 The longest (long) street in the world starts in Toronto, Canada.
2 ______ (wide) street in the world is in Buenos Aires. It is 140 m across.
3 ______ (small) park in the world is 0.29 m$^2$! It is in Portland, Oregon.
4 ______ (crowded) city in the world is Manila, Philippines. It has 41,282 people per km$^2$!
5 ______ (expensive) movie is *Pirates of the Caribbean*. It cost $300 million.
6 ______ (fast) land animal is the cheetah. It can run 120 km/h.

## should / shouldn't

**4 Put the words in order to make sentences or questions.**

1 use / insect spray / You / always / should
You should always use insect spray .
2 take / should / What / on vacation / I
______ ?
3 passport / should / You / your / remember
______ .
4 in winter / shouldn't / He / go there /
______ .
5 go / Should / by airplane / I
______ ?
6 the food / eat / She / shouldn't
______ .

## Study skills

**Using a dictionary**

A dictionary can help you understand new vocabulary. A monolingual English dictionary gives an explanation in English, and some more information.

**1 Look at the dictionary entry for *argue*.**

(1) (2) (3) (4)
★**argue** /ˈɑrgyu/ *verb* **1** [I] **argue (with sb) (about/over sth)** (5) to say things (often angrily) that show that you do not agree with sb about sth: (6) *The people next door are always arguing. I never argue with my husband about money.*

**2 Match the numbers in the dictionary entry with the information below.**

| | | | |
|---|---|---|---|
| Spelling | 1 | Example | ______ |
| Pronunciation | ______ | Stress | ______ |
| Meaning | ______ | Part of speech | ______ |

# 7 Sports world

## Introducing the topic

## Vocabulary

### Sports

**1** 🔊 **Match the photos with the words below. Then listen, check, and repeat.**

| | |
|---|---|
| ☐ basketball | ☐ cycling |
| ☐ field hockey | ☐ gymnastics |
| ☐ snowboarding | ☐ track and field |
| ☐ volleyball | 1 waterskiing |

**2** **Read the Take note! box. Then complete the chart with the sports in exercise 1.**

**Take note!**

*play*, *go*, and *do*

- We use play for ball sports and team sports.
- We use go for sports that end in *-ing*.
- We use do for other sports.

| | |
|---|---|
| **play** | *basketball;* |
| **go** | |
| **do** | |

**3** **Write five sentences about sports that you do or don't do. Use the sports in exercise 1, or your own ideas.**

*I sometimes go cycling after school.*
*I don't play tennis or volleyball.*

## Exploring the topic

# Summer Sports Resolutions

1 I'm going to go cycling with my friends this summer. I have a great new bicycle, and it's really fast! **Kathy, 18**

2 My friend Paul and I like soccer. It's a cool sport! We're going to be in a soccer competition in August. **Jordan, 14**

3 I'm going to play volleyball this summer, but I'm not going to go to the sports center. I'm going to play volleyball at the beach! **Alison, 13**

4 I'm not going to watch TV all summer. I'm going to go running every day. I'm on the track and field team at school. **Jaydee, 15**

5 My brother Mark and I love playing basketball. It's our favorite sport! We're going to play it every day this summer. **Nick, 15**

6 My friend Adam and I are going to go waterskiing at the lake this summer. Adam's dad is going to teach us! **Ben, 15**

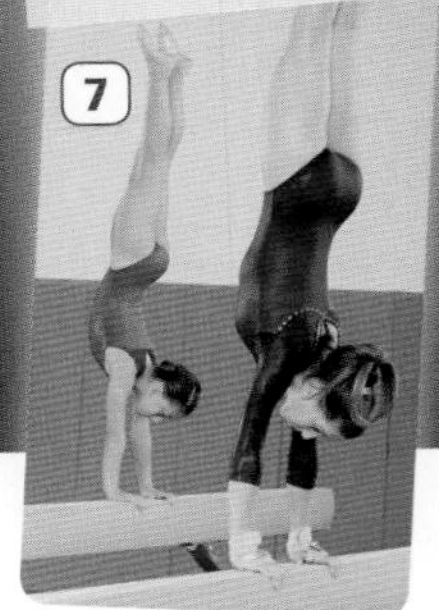

7 I'm going to do gymnastics this summer at a sports camp in Florida. My best friend Tanya is going to come, too! **Carmen, 14**

8 I love snowboarding, but I can't go snowboarding in the summer. There's no snow, so I'm going to go mountainboarding! **Toshi, 16**

## Reading

**1** **Read and listen to the text. Which sport from page 65 is missing?**

**2** **Write the correct names of the people from the text.**

1 He's going to do a water sport.
*Ben*

2 She's going to be at a sports camp.
..........

3 They're going to be in a competition.
..........

4 She isn't going to watch any TV.
..........

5 He's going to play with his brother.
..........

6 She's going to play a ball sport.
..........

**3** **Answer the questions.**

1 When is the soccer competition going to be?
*August*

2 How often is Nick going to play basketball?
..........

3 Who has a new bicycle?
..........

4 Who is going to teach Ben to waterski?
..........

5 Where is Alison going to play volleyball?
..........

6 Who is going to go mountainboarding?
..........

## Grammar

### *be going to* (affirmative / negative)

Talking about plans and resolutions

**1** **Look at the chart.**

| Affirmative | Negative |
|---|---|
| I'**m going to** play volleyball. | I'**m not going to** play volleyball. |
| You'**re going to** do gymnastics. | You **aren't going to** do gymnastics. |
| He'**s going to** go swimming. | She **isn't going to** go swimming. |
| We'**re going to** play tennis. | They **aren't going to** play tennis. |
| You'**re going to** do track and field. | You **aren't going to** do track and field. |
| They'**re going to** go runnning. | They **aren't going to** go running. |

**2** **Fill in the blanks with the correct affirmative form of *be going to*.**

1 You *'re going to* play field hockey tomorrow.
2 Gina .................... go cycling on Friday.
3 I .................... play basketball on the weekend.
4 Those boys .................... go mountainboarding.
5 Keiko .................... do gymnastics on Tuesday.
6 We .................... go swimming tomorrrow.

**3** **Make the sentences in exercise 2 negative.**

1 *You aren't going to play field hockey tomorrow* .
2 .................... .
3 .................... .
4 .................... .
5 .................... .
6 .................... .

**4** **Look at the Sports Camp activities. Write sentences about what the people are going to do (✓), and aren't going to do (✗).**

| | Krista | Brian | Amy |
|---|---|---|---|
| go climbing | ✗ | ✓ | ✗ |
| play basketball | ✗ | ✓ | ✓ |
| go waterskiing | ✓ | ✗ | ✗ |
| go cycling | ✓ | ✗ | ✓ |
| play volleyball | ✗ | ✗ | ✓ |

1 Krista *isn't going to go* climbing.
2 Amy and Brian .................... basketball.
3 Brian .................... waterskiing.
4 Amy .................... cycling.
5 Krista and Brian .................... volleyball.
6 Brian .................... climbing.

**Puzzle** page 89, puzzle 7A

**5** **Over to you!**

**Write affirmative and negative sentences with *be going to* about next weekend. Use the activities below or your own ideas. Then read your sentences to a partner.**

meet friends   play soccer   read a book
ride a horse   watch TV

Student A: I'm going to go surfing on the weekend. And you?
Student B: I'm not going to go surfing. I'm going to watch TV.

# Building the topic

## Vocabulary

### Sports equipment

**1** Look at the website. Fill in the blanks with the words below. Then listen, check, and repeat.

gloves goggles helmet lifejacket pads sneakers ~~tracksuit~~ wetsuit

**SPORTS WEB** *Your online sports store* basket

Swimming >
Track and field >
Winter sports >
Cycling >
Water sports >

Are you going to do track and field? You're going to need a **(1)** tracksuit and a good pair of **(2)** ________ .

Are you going to go cycling? Buy some **(3)** ________ and a good **(4)** ________ for your head.

Are you going to go waterskiing? You're going to need a **(5)** ________ because the ocean is sometimes very cold. And don't forget to wear a **(6)** ________!

Do you want to go snowboarding? Buy some **(7)** ________ for your eyes. You're also going to need **(8)** ________ for your hands.

**2** Circle the correct word.

1 I can run faster when I wear **pads** / **sneakers**.
2 You should wear a **helmet** / **wetsuit** when you go cycling.
3 He sometimes wears a **tracksuit** / **lifejacket** to school.
4 These **goggles** / **gloves** are too small for my hands.
5 Scuba divers wear a **wetsuit** / **tracksuit**.

**3** Match the sentence halves.

1 Goggles
2 A helmet
3 Gloves
4 A lifejacket
5 A wetsuit

a protects your head.
b keeps your body warm.
c keeps you safe in the water.
d protect your hands.
e keep your eyes safe.


Workbook p.W46 → MultiROM

# Grammar

## *be going to* (questions)

Asking questions about plans and resolutions

**1 Look at the chart.**

| Questions | Answers |
| --- | --- |
| **Am** I **going to** do exercise every day? | Yes, I **am**. / No, I**'m not**. |
| **Is** he **going to** practice today? | Yes, he **is**. / No, he **isn't**. |
| **Are** we **going to** wear pads? | Yes, we **are**. / No, we **aren't**. |
| What **is** she **going to** do? | She**'s going to** play tennis. |
| When **are** they **going to** play? | They**'re going to** play today. |

**2 Match the questions and answers.**

1 Is Hiro going to buy a new helmet? *c*
2 What are you going to do tomorrow? ......
3 Are they going to get new goggles? ......
4 Where is Janie going to go this summer? ......
5 Why are we going to buy lifejackets? ......
6 Is your mom going to play tennis? ......

a Because we're going to go waterskiing.
b No, they aren't. They don't have any money.
c No, he isn't. His old one is fine.
d She's going to go to Australia.
e I'm going to go shopping downtown.
f No, she isn't. She hates it.

**3 Look at the pictures. Write questions with *be going to*. Then answer the questions.**

1 Ella / play field hockey?
*Is Ella going to play field hockey* ?
*No, she isn't* .

2 Pedro / go cycling?
...... ?
...... .

3 Ned and Rick / go snowboarding?
...... ?
...... .

4 Ella / go surfing / in the ocean?
...... ?
...... .

5 Pedro / need / a wetsuit?
...... ?
...... .

6 Ned and Rick / wear goggles?
...... ?
...... .

**4 Complete the questions and answers.**

1 A: *Are you going to go* (you / go) to the beach?
B: Yes, I *am* .

2 A: ......
(what / they / do) today?
B: They ...... cycling.

3 A: ......
(when / Rob / play) soccer?
B: He ...... play at four o'clock.

4 A: ......
(Nina / visit) Peru?
B: No, she ...... .

5 A: ......
(what / we / eat) tonight?
B: We ...... eat Italian food.

**Puzzle** page 89, puzzle 7B

**5 Over to you!**

**What are you going to do on the weekend? Ask and answer in class.**

Student A: What are you going to do on the weekend?
Student B: I'm going to play soccer.

# HIT THE SNOW

Are you a snowboarding fan? Meet Celia Miller! She's a professional snowboarder, and she's on the North American Snowboard Team.

Celia lives in Breckenridge, Colorado, in the U.S. She started snowboarding when she was fifteen years old, and now she's famous for her talent and her hard work. Her boyfriend, Chad Otterstrom, is a champion snowboarder, and he's also Celia's biggest fan. People think she's going to be the one to watch next winter.

Celia has a lot of sponsors. For example, companies that make snowboards, sports clothes, sunblock, and energy drinks. She also snowboards for magazine pictures, and in movies! What is she going to do next?

Celia Miller

## Trivia

**Born:** ***Middletown, Connecticut***
**Favorite place to snowboard:** ***Colorado***
**Dream place to visit:** ***Japan***
**Favorite snowboarder:** ***her boyfriend***

Celia has a lot of plans for the future. She's going to keep snowboarding and making movies, and she's going to open a store in her town. It's not going to be a sports store. It's going to be a clothes store with jeans, T-shirts, hats, sunglasses, and jewelry. It sounds like Celia's going to be very busy!

## Reading

**1 Look at the photos and the title of the article. Which sport does the person do?**

**2 Read the text. Circle T (True) or F (False).**

1 Celia was born in Connecticut, in the U.S. T / F
2 She's on the Colorado Snowboarding Team. T / F
3 She's a good snowboarder, and she works hard, too. T / F
4 Some of Celia's sponsors make energy drinks. T / F
5 Celia also takes pictures for a magazine. T / F
6 She's going to open a sports equipment store. T / F

**3 Choose the correct answer.**

1 Celia Miller … when she was a teenager.
a moved to Colorado
b met Chad Otterstrom
c started snowboarding
d drank a lot of energy drinks

2 Some of Celia's sponsors make … .
a movies c surfboards
b drinks d jewelry

3 Celia wants to go to … .
a the Olympic Games c Connecticut
b the store d Japan

4 Celia is going to … next.
a run a business c take pictures
b make hats d make movies

5 Celia is famous for … .
a her movies c her jeans
b her sports clothes d her hard work

 Workbook p.W48

## Listening

### Talking about vacation plans

**1** Look at the Listening skills box.

> **Listening skills**
>
> Predicting main ideas
>
> - When you know the topic of a listening activity, you can try to make predictions about the main ideas.

**2** Nuria is asking Jake about his summer plans. Predict the questions that she is going to ask. Then listen and check.

Nuria's questions:

1 "What are you going to do in **April / July**?"
2 "What are you going to do at **the beach / school**?"
3 "Are you going to go **snowboarding / windsurfing**?"
4 "Do you have your own **skis / tracksuit**?"
5 "Are you going to need a **helmet / wetsuit**?"

**3** Listen to the conversation again. Answer the questions.

1 Where is Jake going to go in July?
*He's going to go to the beach in Tampa, Florida*.
2 Which three sports is he going to do?
.
3 When did Jake get his new skis?
.
4 What is Jake going to buy at the sports store?
.
5 When are Nuria and Jake going to go shopping?
.

## Speaking

### Talking about plans

**1** Listen and read.

Chester: What are you going to do in August?
Jordan: I'm going to go camping. What about you?
Chester: I'm not going to go camping. I'm going to go to the beach.
Jordan: That's great! Are you going to go waterskiing?
Chester: Yes! And I'm going to take scuba diving lessons, too!

**2** Look at the Pronunciation box. Listen to the examples. Then listen again and repeat.

> **Pronunciation**
>
> /g/ and /ŋ/ sounds

| /g/ | /ŋ/ |
|---|---|
| go | going |
| August | waterskiing |
| great | camping |

**3** Listen to the sentences. Then complete the chart with the underlined words.

1 Greg didn't bring any green apples.
2 Does Maggie know any good songs?

| /g/ | /ŋ/ |
|---|---|
| *Greg*, | *bring*, |

**4** Practice the dialogue in exercise 1.

**5** Now change the words in blue. Write a new dialogue. Then practice the dialogue in class.

# Round-up

## Writing
### Summer sports plans

**1** **Look at the Writing skills box.**

**Writing skills**

*also* and *too*

- **We use *also* and *too* to add extra information.**
  Waterpolo is fun. It's also exciting.
  I like skiing. I also like snowboarding.
  He needs a helmet. He needs pads, too.

**Now read Sovann's e-mail. Circle the words *also* and *too* in the e-mail.**

**2** **Complete the chart with Sovann's information.**

| Sovann's summer plans | |
|---|---|
| What's his favorite summer sport? | waterskiing |
| Why does he like it? | |
| Where is he going to do the sport this summer? | |
| What other sports is he going to do? | |
| What new equipment is he going to need? | |

**3** **Make a chart with your own answers for the Summer Sports Plans contest.**

**SPORTS WEB**

**SUMMER SPORTS PLANS!**

**Send us an e-mail about your summer sports plans and you can win a prize!**

Hello!

My name's Sovann Pok, and I'm from Phnom Penh, in Cambodia.

My favorite summer sport is waterskiing. I like waterskiing because it's a fast, exciting sport. I'm very good at it, too!

This summer, I'm going to go waterskiing with my family in Sihanoukville. It's a popular beach town in Cambodia.

I'm going to go scuba diving, too. It's going to be my first time! I'm also going to go surfing with my dad. He's going to teach me!

Before we go on vacation, I'm going to get a lifejacket. I need a new wetsuit, too. My old wetsuit isn't big enough! I also need some new goggles. My parents are going to buy everything from Sports Web, of course! ☺

Sincerely,

Sovann Pok

**4** **Write an e-mail for the Summer Sports Plans contest. Use your chart and Sovann's e-mail to help you.**

## I can ...

**1** **Write sentences about your next vacation.**

1 I'm not going to go to the beach.
2 ______.
3 ______.
4 ______.

**I can describe my future plans.**
Yes, I can. ☐ I need more practice. ☐

**2** **Match the questions with the answers.**

1 What are you going to do on Saturday? c
2 Are your parents going to buy a new car? ____
3 Are we going to see Peter tonight? ____

a Yes, they are. It's expensive!
b No, we aren't. He's sick.
c I'm going to go to the movies with Amy.

**I can ask questions about plans and resolutions.**
Yes, I can. ☐ I need more practice. ☐

# 8 Having fun

## Introducing the topic

## Vocabulary

### Fun events

**1** **Match the photos with the words below. Then listen, check, and repeat.**

| | |
|---|---|
| ☐ art exhibition | ☐ baseball game |
| ☐ birthday party | ☐ fashion show |
| 1 music festival | ☐ parade |
| ☐ picnic | ☐ stage play |

**2** **Fill in the blanks with the events in exercise 1.**

1 The actors in that *stage play* are very funny!
2 We're making a salad for the ______ tomorrow.
3 A lot of people were in the ______. It was two kilometers long!
4 My favorite band is playing at the ______ this weekend.
5 There was an ______ of paintings at our school.
6 Which teams are playing in the ______ tonight?
7 I'm going to a ______ at the shopping mall. I love clothes!
8 Amy's having a ______ next Friday. She's going to be sixteen.

**3** **Write five sentences about fun events you're going to attend. You can use the events in exercise 1, or your own ideas.**

*I'm going to go to a birthday party on Saturday.*

# Exploring the topic

## Friend finder

You are in **the chatroom**

**Angie**
Hi, Kyra! What are you doing next Saturday?

**Kyra**
Hi, Angie! I'm going to a modern art exhibition at the museum. Do you want to come with me?

**Angie**
I'm not sure. I have a karate lesson at 9 a.m. What time are you going to the museum?

**Kyra**
At 11 a.m, but I can only stay for a couple of hours. Then I'm meeting Jess and Tomoko. We're having a picnic in the park at 2 p.m.

**Angie**
Well, I can go to the museum with you, but I can't go to the park. My little sister is having a birthday party in the afternoon, and I have to help my parents.

**Kyra**
That's too bad! What about in the evening? Are you staying home?

**Angie**
No, I'm not. Why? Are you doing anything special?

**Kyra**
Well, there's a Caribbean music festival downtown. Four different bands are playing. Maybe we can get tickets. There's going to be a street market, too, so we can have Caribbean food for dinner. What do you think?

**Angie**
I think that's a great idea. I can't wait!

Reply

## Reading

**1** **Read and listen to the online chat. Are Angie and Kyra going to see each other on Saturday evening?**

**2** **Read the text. Circle T (True) or F (False).**

1 Kyra is going to an art exhibition in the park. T / (F)
2 Kyra is going to the exhibition at 11 a.m. T / F
3 Tomoko and Jess are going to the museum. T / F
4 Angie's brother is having a birthday party. T / F
5 Kyra isn't staying home in the evening. T / F
6 Five bands are playing on Saturday evening. T / F

**3** **Answer the questions. Write full sentences.**

1 What is Angie doing before the art exhibition?
*She has a karate lesson* .
2 How long is Kyra going to be at the museum?
…… .
3 What is Kyra doing in the park at 2 p.m.?
…… .
4 What does Angie have to do on Saturday afternoon?
…… .
5 What is happening downtown in the evening?
…… .
6 Where are the girls having dinner on Saturday?
……
…… .

# Grammar

## Present progressive for the future

Talking about appointments and arrangements

**1** **Look at the chart.**

| Affirmative | Negative |
|---|---|
| I'**m meeting** Paulo on Friday. | I'**m not meeting** Sam on Friday. |
| He'**s going** to a concert later. | He **isn't going** to a party later. |
| **Questions** | **Answers** |
| **Are** you **going** to the theater tonight? | Yes, **I am**. / No, **I'm not**. |
| What time **are** you **taking** the bus? | I'**m taking** the bus at six o'clock. |

**2** **Chad is a pop star. Look at his agenda and complete the sentences. Use the affirmative or negative form of the present progressive.**

1 On Monday morning, Chad *is doing* an interview with Pop News.
2 He .................... to an art exhibition on Monday evening.
3 He .................... dinner with Steven on Tuesday evening.
4 On Wednesday morning, Chad .................... home.
5 He .................... his friend Kristin in the evening.
6 On Thursday, Chad .................... to Los Angeles.

**3** **Complete the questions about Chad's appointments. Use the correct form of the present progressive. Then write the answers.**

1 *Is Chad having* (Chad / have) dinner with Lucy on Monday? *No, he isn't*.
2 What .................... (he / do) on Tuesday morning? ....................
....................
3 .................... (Chad and Katy / go) to a music festival on Wednesday?
.................... .
4 Where ....................
(Kristin and Chad / meet) on Wednesday?
....................
.................... .
5 .................... (Jorge / play) tennis with Chad this week? .................... .
6 When .................... (Chad / have) a party?
....................
.................... .

**Puzzle** page 89, puzzle 8A

**4** **Over to you!**

**What are you doing this weekend? Ask and answer in class.**

Student A: What are you doing on Saturday morning?
Student B: I'm playing tennis with Martin. And you?

# Building the topic

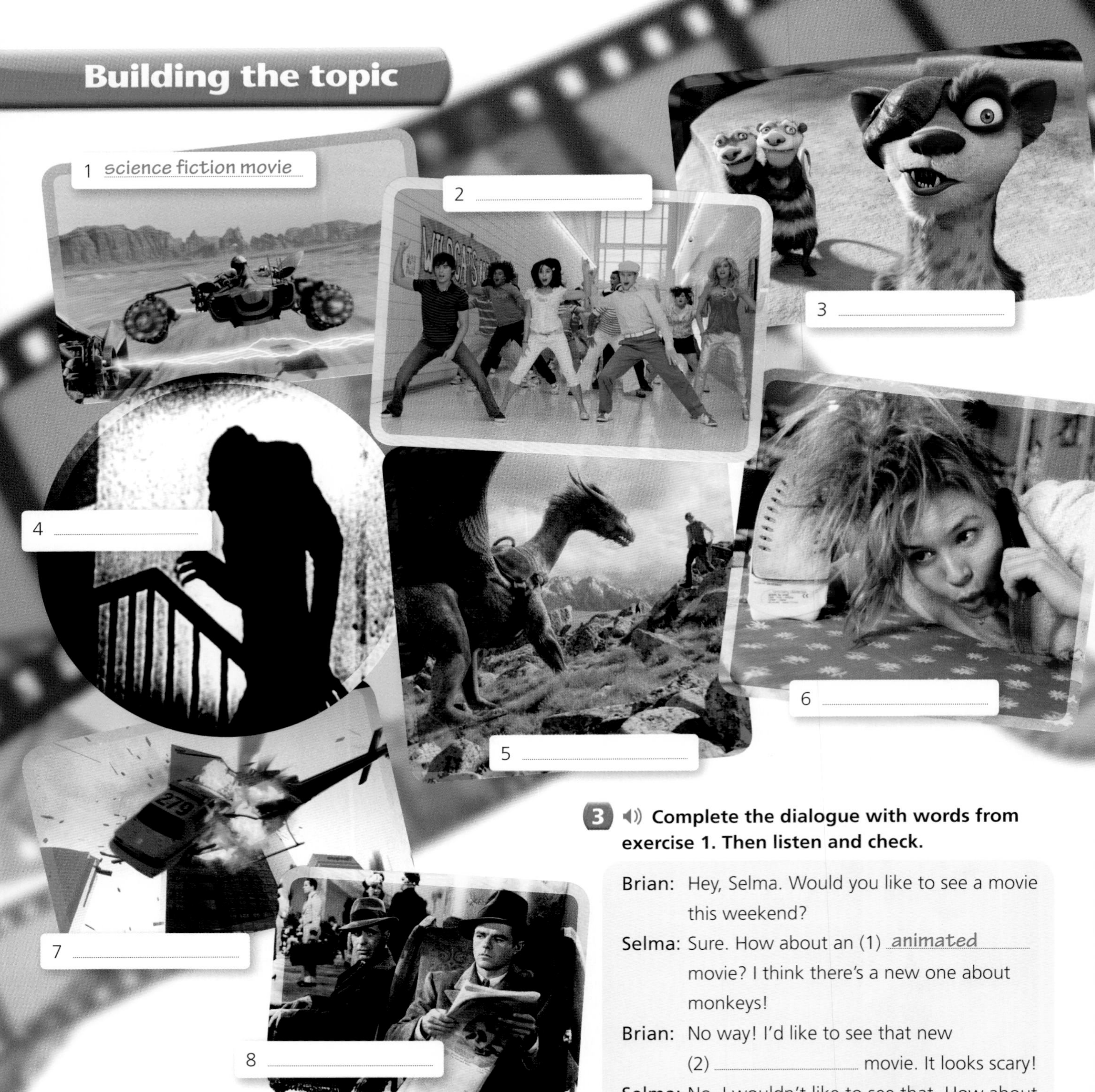


## Vocabulary

### Kinds of movies

**1** **Label the pictures with the words below. Then listen, check, and repeat.**

action movie   animated movie   comedy
fantasy movie   horror movie   musical
mystery   ~~science fiction movie~~

**2** **Write an example for each kind of movie in exercise 1. Then compare your list with a friend.**

*Star Wars is a science fiction movie.*

**3** **Complete the dialogue with words from exercise 1. Then listen and check.**

**Brian:** Hey, Selma. Would you like to see a movie this weekend?

**Selma:** Sure. How about an (1) *animated* movie? I think there's a new one about monkeys!

**Brian:** No way! I'd like to see that new (2) ________ movie. It looks scary!

**Selma:** No, I wouldn't like to see that. How about a (3) ________ movie? There's a new *Harry Potter* movie at the movie theater.

**Brian:** No, I already saw that last week. There's a (4) ________ movie about aliens. Would you like to see it?

**Selma:** Hmm, no thanks. I don't like aliens. But how about that new (5) ________ movie with Shia LaBeouf? It looks exciting.

**Brian:** OK. What time is it on?

**Selma:** I'm not sure. Let's look on the Internet.

## Grammar

### *I'd like ... / Would you like ...?*

Making requests and offers

**1** **Look at the chart.**

| Affirmative + infinitive | Questions and answers |
|---|---|
| I**'d like** to go to the movies. | **Would** you **like** to go to the movies? |
| We**'d like** to see a comedy. | **Would** you **like** to see a comedy? |
| | Yes, please. / No, thanks. |

**2** **Put the words in order to make sentences or questions.**

1 movie / to see / What / would / like / you
What movie would you like to see ?

2 a birthday party / I / to have / like / would
.................................................... .

3 tennis / to / Would / play / like / you
.................................................... ?

4 you / would / to have / lunch / Where / like
.................................................... ?

5 would / to / We / a concert / like / to go
.................................................... .

6 like / Would / to drink / you / juice / some
.................................................... ?

**3** **Look at the chart.**

| Affirmative + noun | Questions and answers |
|---|---|
| I**'d like** a hamburger. | **Would** you **like** a hamburger? |
| They**'d like** two drinks. | **Would** they **like** two drinks? |
| She**'d like** some chocolate. | **Would** she **like** some chocolate? |
| | Yes, please. / No, thanks. |

**4** **Fill in the blanks with the correct form of *would like*.**

1 "We 'd like some popcorn, please."

2 She .................... an ice cream.

3 ".................... you .................... two tickets?"

4 They .................... bigger seats.

5 ".................... you .................... some potato chips?"

6 He .................... a big drink.

**5** **Write offers. Use the words below.**

a cold drink  a new bike  a pen  some help
some magazines  ~~some pizza~~

1 A: I'm hungry.
B: Would you like some pizza ?

2 A: I'm thirsty.
B: .................................................... ?

3 A: I don't have anything to read.
B: .................................................... ?

4 A: I want to write a note.
B: .................................................... ?

5 A: I can't carry these books!
B: .................................................... ?

6 A: It's my birthday next week.
B: .................................................... ?

**Puzzle** page 89, puzzle 8B

**6** **Over to you!**

**Think of five different offers. Use *Would you like ...?* Then make and answer offers in class.**

Student A: Would you like a cup of coffee?
Student B: No, thanks. Would you like to go to a party?
Student A: Yes, please.

# Saturday events this month

**1 Saturday May 6th: *Hairspray!***

Did you see the musical *Hairspray*, with John Travolta and Zac Efron? Would you like to see the stage play, too? The school Drama Club is performing *Hairspray* at the Central Theater at 8 p.m. Tickets cost ten dollars at the door, but you can also buy them online for only eight dollars.

**2 Saturday May 13th: *Fashion Show***

Fashion fans are going to love this event. Ten stores are organizing a fashion show at the shopping mall in the afternoon. Tickets are only five dollars, and they're using the money to buy uniforms for our school soccer team. Would you like to be a model in the show? They're going to need six girls and six boys.

**3 Saturday May 20th: *Movie Marathon***

The Movie Club is having a *Twilight* Movie Marathon from 10 a.m. to 11 p.m. in the school gym. Dress as your favorite *Twilight* character, and win a prize for the best costume! The Movie Club is selling drinks and snacks all day, but you can also bring your own food. Tickets only cost one dollar for each movie.

**4 Saturday May 27th: *Teen Art Exhibition***

Are you an artist? Would you like to show your work? The Youth Center is organizing a free art exhibition in the morning. You can bring a drawing, a painting, or a photograph. The Youth Center is giving a prize for the best teen artist – a trip to New York City to visit the Museum of Modern Art!

## Reading

**1 Read the newspaper page quickly. Which events are happening at these locations?**

a in the school gym *a movie marathon*
b at the Youth Center ……
c at the shopping mall ……
d at the theater ……

**2 Read again. Write the number of the event.**

1 They're selling food and drinks. *3*
2 The tickets cost five dollars. ……
3 It's only happening in the morning. ……
4 You can buy your tickets online. ……
5 You can win a prize. …… and ……
6 They're looking for people to help. ……

**3 Choose the correct answer.**

1 You can buy tickets for Hairspray … .
a at Drama Club
b on the stage
(c) on the Internet
d for nine dollars

2 The fashion show is going to give the money to … .
a the shopping mall
b a sports team
c the Drama Club
d local stores

3 You can buy … at the Movie Marathon.
a a costume
b food
c the *Twilight* movies
d a prize

4 You have to … to enter the art exhibition.
a be a painter
b visit a museum
c pay
d be creative

**4 Think about it**

**Which of the events would you like to go to? What events are happening at your school this month?**


Workbook p.W54

## Listening

### Talking about arrangements

**1 Listen to the conversation. What is Chloe's problem?**

a She's bored.
b She's tired.
c She's hungry.
d She's sick.

**2 Listen again. Circle the correct word.**

1 Noah is meeting Jenny in the **morning** / **afternoon**.
2 They're going to a **football** / **basketball** game.
3 Chloe wants to go **out** / **home** after the game.
4 They're going to go out for **lunch** / **dinner**.
5 Noah's going to meet Chloe **before** / **after** he meets Jenny.

**3 Circle the correct answer.**

1 Where is Noah meeting Jenny?
   a at a café
   b at the football game
   c at Chloe's house
   d at a restaurant
2 What does Chloe think about football?
   a She loves it.
   b She likes it.
   c She doesn't like it.
   d She hates it.
3 Where is the restaurant?
   a on Park Street
   b on Main Street
   c on River Street
   d on Center Street
4 What time is Jenny meeting Noah?
   a at one o'clock
   b at one thirty
   c at two o'clock
   d at two thirty

## Speaking

### Making arrangements

**1 Listen and read.**

Jordan: What are you doing tonight?
Gabby: I'm going to a fashion show with Mariella.
Jordan: Cool! What about tomorrow afternoon?
Gabby: I'm going to a baseball game with Chester. Would you like to come with us?
Jordan: Sure, I'd love to!
Gabby: Great! We're meeting at my house at one o'clock.
Jordan: OK. See you then!

**2 Look at the Pronunciation box. Listen to the examples. Then listen again and repeat.**

**Pronunciation**

*would you*

- **In conversation, we pronounce *would you* as /wʊdʒu/.**

Would you like to come with us?
What would you like to do?

**3 Listen and repeat. Then practice the sentences.**

1 Would you like to go with us?
2 Where would you like to go?
3 Would you like to see a movie?
4 What would you like to see?

**4 Practice the dialogue in exercise 1.**

**5 Now change the words in blue. Write a new dialogue. Then practice the dialogue in class.**

# Round-up

## Writing

### An invitation

**1 Read Patricia's e-mail to Mia. Check (✓) the activities she is doing for her birthday.**

a going to a music festival ☐
b having a party ☐
c having a picnic ☐
d going to the movie theater ☐

Hi, Mia!

I have some great news! Next Saturday is my 15th birthday, (so) I'm having a party! Would you like to come?

I'm having the party at my house. It's going to start at three o'clock in the afternoon. It's a pool party, so you should bring your swimsuit. We're making hamburgers for dinner, and my parents are ordering pizza, too.

In the evening, it's going to be too cold to swim, so we're going to the movie theater. I'd like to see that new movie *Horror Hotel*, but my parents say it's too scary. What would you like to see? How about that musical *Summer Camp*? I think it looks good.

I really hope you can come to the party. Send me an e-mail soon!

Love,

Patricia

**2 Fill in the chart with information from Patricia's e-mail.**

| Patricia's invitation | |
|---|---|
| Type of party | *birthday / pool party* |
| Location | |
| Starting time | |
| Afternoon activity | |
| Dinner foods | |
| Evening activity | |

**3 Look at the Writing skills box.**

**Writing skills**

*so*

- **We use *so* to join ideas and talk about results.**
  It's sunny today. I'm going to the beach.
  It's sunny today, so I'm going to the beach.

**Now circle examples of *so* in the text.**

**4 Imagine you are having a birthday party. Make a chart like the one in exercise 2.**

**5 Write an invitation to a friend. Use Patricia's e-mail and your chart to help you.**

## I can ...

**1 Write questions and answers to describe your future arrangements.**

1 *Are you meeting your friends this week* ?
(meet your friends) *No, I'm not* .

2 ________________
(play tennis) on the weekend? ________ .

3 ________________
(study) tonight? ________ .

**I can ask and answer questions about my future arrangements.**
Yes, I can. ☐ I need more practice. ☐

**2 Unscramble the questions and answer them.**

1 to / Would / lunch / have / like / you
*Would you like to have lunch*? *Yes, please* .

2 like / to / Would / you / a / see / movie
________________ ?
________ .

3 like / chocolate / Would / some / you
________________ ?
________ .

**I can make requests and offers.**
Yes, I can. ☐ I need more practice. ☐

# D Review

## Vocabulary

### Sports

**1** Complete the names of the sports.

1 snowboarding
2 _o_e_a_
3 _a_e_a_
4 ___i_
5 _a_a_ie_
6 _ie_ _o_ey
7 __a_i_
8 _a_e_ii_

### Sports equipment

**2** Match the definitions with the words below.

gloves ~~goggles~~ helmet lifejacket pads
sneakers tracksuit wetsuit

1 You wear them to protect your eyes. goggles
2 You wear it when you go running. ........
3 They warm your hands when it's cold. ........
4 It's hard and you wear it on your head. ........
5 You should always wear it in a canoe. ........
6 You wear them on your feet when you play tennis. ........
7 You need them when you go skateboarding. ........
8 It keeps your body warm in cold water. ........

### Fun events

**3** Label the fun events.

1 a music festival
2 a ........
3 an ........
4 a ........
5 a ........
6 a ........
7 a ........
8 a ........

### Kinds of movies

**4** Match the sentence halves.

1 I like action movies — d
2 That new comedy
3 There were some
4 I saw a fantasy
5 That science fiction
6 It was a mystery
7 *Toy Story* is my
8 That horror movie

a good songs in that musical.
b is too scary for children.
c movie was about a robot.
d because they're exciting.
e about a famous detective.
f favorite animated movie.
g was really funny!
h movie called *Dragons 2*.

Review

## Grammar

### *be going to* (affirmative and negative)

**1 Fill in the blanks with the affirmative and negative forms of *be going to*.**

1 We *are going to* do gymnastics later. (✓)
2 She ................ meet us for lunch. (✗)
3 I ................ play tennis this summer. (✓)
4 You ................ buy a lifejacket. (✗)
5 He ................ go cycling tonight. (✓)
6 They ................ get some pads. (✓)
7 I ................ go snowboarding. (✗)

### *be going to* (questions)

**2 Lori and Kevin are going to do a lot of sport this summer. Look at their plans and then write questions and answers.**

| | Lori | Kevin |
|---|---|---|
| wake up early | ✓ | ✓ |
| go cycling | ✗ | ✓ |
| go swimming at the beach | ✓ | ✗ |
| do karate | ✗ | ✓ |
| go running in the evening | ✓ | ✓ |
| go to bed early | ✓ | ✓ |

1 they / wake up early
*Are they going to wake up early* ?
*Yes, they are* .
2 Kevin / go cycling
................ ?
................ .
3 Where / Lori / go swimming
................ ?
................ .
4 Lori / do karate
................ ?
................ .
5 When / Kevin / go running
................ ?
................ .
6 they / go to bed early
................ ?
................ .

### Present progressive for the future

**3 Fill in the blanks with the correct form of the present progressive to complete Maly's plans for Saturday.**

1 Maly *is meeting* Ada for breakfast. (meet)
2 She ................ to the gym at 10 a.m. (not go)
3 Maly ................ her grandmother at 11 a.m. (visit)
4 Ben and Maly ................ lunch together. (have)
5 Maly ................ to a fashion show. (not go)
6 She and Suzy ................ a movie. (not see)

### *Would you like ...?*

**4 Write questions with *Would you like ...?* Then answer the questions.**

1 some milk (✓)
*Would you like some milk* ? *Yes, please* .
2 a hamburger (✗)
................ ? ................ .
3 to go dancing (✓)
................ ? ................ .
4 some chocolate (✗)
................ ? ................ .
5 to listen to some music (✓)
................ ?
................ .
6 a new cell phone (✗)
................ ? ................ .

### Study skills

**Word families**

When you learn a new word, look for it in your dictionary. You can find more words in the same "word family".

**1 Use your dictionary to complete the chart below.**

| Verb | Adjective | Noun |
|---|---|---|
| create | creative | creation |
| organize | 1 *organized* | 2 ................ |
| 3 ................ | competitive | 4 ................ |
| 5 ................ | 6 ................ | protection |
| animate | 7 ................ | 8 ................ |

# engage magazine 1

## puzzle 1A

Circle the five extra letters in each sentence. Use the extra letters to make a secret question. Then answer the question.

1 Rewadinghmagaazinesistinterdesting.
Reading magazines is interesting.

2 Usingotheycomopuuterisdfun.

3 Thesotudentsiloveplayinngsyoccero.

4 Weudontlikershopfpingforrclotehes.

5 Leistentingtomusiicisnotmboreing.

Secret question: What ... ?

## puzzle 1B

Unscramble and order the words. Then match them with the pictures. Which picture is extra?

1 sargs / tcu / het
cut the grass – C

2 alcen / omor / royu

3 eth / tse / balet

4 uyro / ebd / akem

5 sisdeh / hasw / teh

## puzzle 2A

Match the people with the places and the kinds of transportation. Then complete the sentences.

bus · Brazil · Argentina · motorcycle · sailboat · Thailand · Honduras · airplane · helicopter · Cambodia · Mexico · train · ferry · car · France · Singapore

1 Bea is going to Brazil by bus.
2 Ayrton is going to Argentina by airplane.
3 Telma is going to ______ by ______.
4 Felipe ______ by ______.
5 Sandra ______ by ______.
6 Harry ______ by ______.
7 Monica ______ by ______.
8 Calvin ______ by ______.

## puzzle 2B

Find and circle ten adjectives. Then complete the sentences.

| | | | | | | | | | |
|---|---|---|---|---|---|---|---|---|---|
| → | S | A | B | L | E | R | T | A | B |
| F | A | T | R | A | F | O | F | E | L |
| E | N | F | O | S | T | O | M | Q | U |
| I | O | M | O | A | D | C | N | E | I |
| S | Y | T | C | N | G | Y | U | T | S |
| I | D | L | U | R | E | S | A | O | L |
| F | F | I | C | O | U | S | E | W | → |

1 That old sailboat is too dangerous. It's going to sink!
2 Cars are too ______ for me. I like airplanes because they're fast.
3 I'm not good at skateboarding. It's too ______ for me.
4 Buses are too ______. I never have enough room!
5 I can't hear you very well. That motorcycle is too ______.

# PROJECT 1

**1** **Read the description. Match the headings with the paragraphs.**

> What are the rules?
> What do you like doing there?
> When can you go there?
> ~~Where is it?~~

## OUR YOUTH CLUB

1 *Where is it?*
My name is Miles. I'm fifteen years old. I live in Bristol, in the U.K. Our youth club is in an old school near my house. Twelve- to nineteen-year-olds can go there to meet friends, hang out, and do a lot of different activities.

2 ____________________
I often meet my friends at the club to play basketball and computer games. I also do karate twice a week. I'm practicing for my orange belt! My little sister Alana has art classes at the club. She loves painting and drawing. She also likes playing ping pong there with her friends.

3 ____________________
You can go to the club from Monday to Thursday. The club doesn't open until 3 p.m. and you can't stay later than 10 p.m. Most of the activities are twice a week, for example, on Monday and Wednesday or on Tuesday and Thursday. There are sometimes group trips on the weekends, too. Last Saturday, I went to the science museum with a group of people. It was interesting!

4 ____________________
There's a room where you can watch TV or play games, but you can't make a lot of noise. There's a small library, too. You can study and take out books, but you can't talk. You have to be quiet. The club also has a computer room, but there are only ten computers. You have to wait your turn, and you can't use the computer for a very long time.

**2** **Think about a youth club or another fun place in your area. Take notes. Use the questions in exercise 1.**

**3** **Write about your fun place on a poster. Use Miles's model to help you. Find photos or draw pictures to decorate your poster.**

**4** **Present your poster to the class.**

# engage magazine 2

## puzzle 3A

Look at the people at the bus stop. Read the clues and guess their identities.

Someone was talking on a cell phone behind Chris.
The person behind Lee was eating an ice cream.
Someone was reading a newspaper in front of Rudi.
The person in front of Fran was holding an umbrella.

## puzzle 3B

READ THE DESCRIPTIONS AND LOOK AT THE PICTURE. THEN LABEL THE PEOPLE.

- *Was Dana holding a present?* NO, SHE WASN'T.
- *Was Natalie sitting down?* YES, SHE WAS.
- *Was John walking?* NO, HE WASN'T.
- *Was Maria carrying a bag?* YES, SHE WAS.
- *Was Abel wearing green?* YES, HE WAS.
- *Was Luisa wearing blue?* NO, SHE WASN'T.
- *Was Brittany shaking hands?* YES, SHE WAS.

## puzzle 4A

Look at the Morse code table. Use the code and write the names of the natural disasters.

| A | B | C | D | E | F | G | H | I |
|---|---|---|---|---|---|---|---|---|
| •- | -••• | -•-• | -•• | • | ••-• | --• | •••• | •• |
| J | K | L | M | N | O | P | Q | R |
| •--- | -•- | •-•• | -- | -• | --- | •--• | --•- | •-• |
| S | T | U | V | W | X | Y | Z | |
| ••• | - | ••- | •••- | •-- | -••- | -•-- | --•• | |

1 ••-• •-•• --- --- -•• FLOOD
2 - ••• ••- -• •- -- •• ..........
3 • •- •-• - •••• --•- ••- •- -•- • ..........
4 -••• •-•• •• --•• --•• •- •-• -•• ..........
5 •••• ••- •-• •-• •• -•-• •- -• • ..........

## puzzle 4B

**Break the code and write the secret sentence.**

| A | B | C | D | E | F | G | H | I |
|---|---|---|---|---|---|---|---|---|
| 9 | 18 | X | | 2 | X | | | |
| J | K | L | M | N | O | P | Q | R |
| X | X | 24 | X | X | 25 | 22 | X | |
| S | T | U | V | W | X | Y | Z | |
| | 14 | | X | X | X | 1 | X | |

T O B Y   P L A ___ ___   ___ ___ E
14 25 18 1   22 24 9 1 11   14 17 2

___ ___ ___ ___ ___ ___   ___ ___ ___ ___ ___ ___!
15 8 4 14 9 20   24 25 8 13 24 1

# PROJECT 2

**1** **Read Tate's description of an incredible experience. Then match the headings with the paragraphs.**

| | |
|---|---|
| ~~When and where did it happen?~~ | What were you doing at first? |
| What happened in the end? | What did you do after that? |
| What did you see, hear, and feel? | |

## An Amazing Experience

1 When and where did it happen?
I had an incredible experience last spring. It was a Saturday afternoon, and I was at my uncle's farm. It's near Tulsa, Oklahoma, in the U.S.

2 ______________________
It was about four o'clock in the afternoon. I was walking in the field, when the sky became very dark and cloudy. It happened very quickly!

3 ______________________
The wind started blowing very hard. It was really noisy! Then I looked up and saw something strange. It was a big, black cloud, and it was coming down to the ground. It was a tornado! I was really scared!

4 ______________________
I quickly ran back to the house. My parents and my uncle were looking for me. They were shouting, but I couldn't understand what they were saying.

5 ______________________
We went to hide in a special basement under the house. In the end, the wind stopped blowing, and the sun came out again. We were safe, and very lucky!

**2** **Think about an incredible experience in your life. Take notes about what happened. Use the questions in exercise 1.**

**3** **Write your story on a poster. Find photos or draw pictures to decorate your poster.**

**4** **Present your poster and story to the class.**

# engage magazine 3

## puzzle 5A

**Read the descriptions and answer the questions.**

Mario is 1.80 m tall. David is shorter than Mario, but he is taller than Peter. Andy is taller than Mario, but he is shorter than Carl. Tim and Steven are the same height. They are taller than Andy and Carl.

1 Who are taller than everyone else?

2 Who is shorter than everyone else?

## puzzle 5B

**Unscramble the letters to make personality adjectives. Use the letters on colored squares to make a secret question. Then answer the question.**

| | | | | | | | | | | | |
|---|---|---|---|---|---|---|---|---|---|---|---|
| fuhllpe | H | E | L | P | F | U | L | | | | |
| geazidsornid | | | | | | | | | | | |
| visetsnie | | | | | | | | | | | |
| lehurcef | | | | | | | | | | | |
| liekavtat | | | | | | | | | | | |
| bialosec | | | | | | | | | | | |
| tivoecempti | | | | | | | | | | | |

## puzzle 6A

**Order the letters with the same color. Complete the questions about your country. Then answer them.**

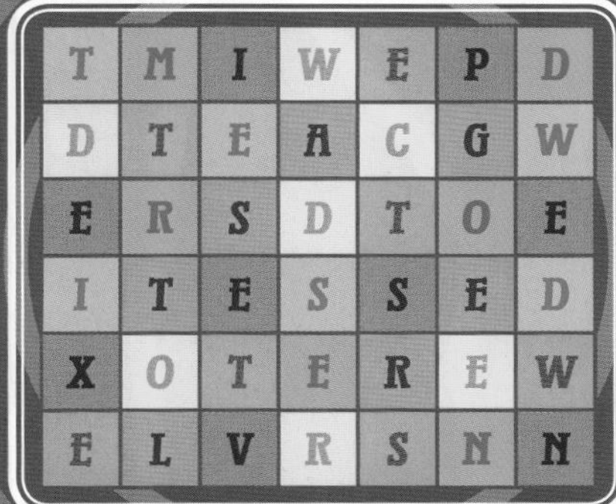

| | | | | | | |
|---|---|---|---|---|---|---|
| T | M | I | W | E | P | D |
| D | T | E | A | C | G | W |
| E | R | S | D | T | O | E |
| I | T | E | S | S | E | D |
| X | O | T | E | R | E | W |
| E | L | V | R | S | N | N |

1 What is the most modern building in your country?

2 What is the ______ river?

3 What is the most ______ city?

4 What is the most ______ food?

5 What is the ______ place?

6 What is the ______ lake?

## puzzle 6B

**Change the underlined words and rewrite the sentences.**

1 There are a lot of mosquitoes. I need some <u>swimsuit</u>.
*There are a lot of mosquitoes. I need some insect spray.*

2 We took some great photos with our new <u>passport</u>.

3 Pamela was wearing her new <u>hiking boots</u> at the pool.

4 My feet hurt. I think my <u>insect spray</u> are too small!

5 Brendan was reading his <u>e-ticket</u> during the flight.

6 You look really young in your <u>camera</u> photo.

7 Oh no! I can't get on the airplane. I forgot my <u>sunblock</u>!

8 You should put on some <u>guidebook</u>. Your nose is red!

# PROJECT 3

**1** Read about Neela's style. Match the headings with the paragraphs.

| My personality | ~~My hair~~ | My favorite place | My clothes |
|---|---|---|---|

# My Style

1 My hair

I have dark brown hair. It's naturally curly, but I often wear it straight. Right now, my hair is really long, but I usually have it shorter in the summer when the weather is hotter. I want to dye my hair purple someday for fun, but my mom says I can't. ☹

2 ..............................

I often wear tight pants, and T-shirts with slogans on them. I like wearing sneakers, because they're comfortable. I love warm, cheerful colors – like red, orange, and yellow – because they make me feel good. I never wear grey – it's too depressing!

3 ..............................

I'm a very sociable person. I love meeting friends, but some people say I'm too talkative. I'm not very organized – my bedroom is a disaster, and I often forget my homework. I'm very creative. I love painting and drawing, and I play the guitar, too.

4 ..............................

I love warm weather and the beach, so my favorite place is Los Angeles, California. My grandparents live there, and I visit them in the summer. I love Los Angeles because it's big and modern, and the most famous and fashionable people live there.

**2** Find a photo that shows your style. Take notes about your style. Use the headings in exercise 1.

**3** Write about your style on a poster. Use Neela's description to help you.

**4** Present your poster to the class.

# engage magazine 4

## puzzle 7A

1 Kiet *is* going *to go cycling* .
2 Carmen ........ going ........ .
3 Mei and Lan ........ going ........ .
4 Kylee ........ going ........ .
5 Maru ........ going ........ .
6 Alec and Damon ........ going ........ .

## puzzle 7B

Find eight names of sports equipment in the puzzle. Find the secret question and answer it.

| | | | | | | | | | |
|---|---|---|---|---|---|---|---|---|---|
| L | A | R | E | Y | O | H | U | G | O |
| I | I | N | G | T | E | O | S | T | B |
| F | U | Y | S | L | O | M | R | S | E |
| E | W | N | M | E | W | A | E | D | S |
| J | E | E | P | O | C | L | K | A | R |
| A | T | T | S | K | G | E | A | P | Q |
| C | S | U | S | G | I | P | E | M | E |
| K | U | U | O | N | T | O | N | N | T |
| E | I | G | L | O | V | E | S | H | E |
| T | T | W | E | E | K | E | N | D | ? |

**Secret question:**

*Are you* ........

## puzzle 8A

**Copy alternate letters to make questions about next weekend. Use all of the letters. Then answer the questions.**

**1** ANRAERYTOEUXGHOIIBNIGTTIOOAN?
Are you *going to an art exhibition* ?

**2** AARVEIYNOGUARPFOROILEPNADRSTHY?
........ ?

**3** IASMTEHTEHRIESAWSEOECKCEENRDG?
........ ?

**4** AIRCENYIOCUIHNATVHIENPGAARPK?
........ ?

## puzzle 8B

Use the code to write the sentences.

| A | B | C | D | E | F | G | H | I |
|---|---|---|---|---|---|---|---|---|
| 6 | 7 | 8 | 9 | 10 | 11 | 12 | 13 | 14 |
| J | K | L | M | N | O | P | Q | R |
| 15 | 16 | 17 | 18 | 19 | 20 | 21 | 22 | 23 |
| S | T | U | V | W | X | Y | Z | |
| 24 | 25 | 26 | 1 | 2 | 3 | 4 | 5 | |

**1** We'd like to ___ ___ ___ (24 10 10) ___ ___ (6 19) ___ ___ ___ ___ ___ ___ (6 8 25 14 20 19) movie.

**2** I'd like ___ ___ ___ ___ (24 20 18 10) ___ ___ ___ ___ ___ ___ ___ (21 20 21 8 20 23 19), please.

**3** Would you like ___ (6) ___ ___ ___ (19 10 2) ___ (6) ___ ___ ___ (19 10 2) ___ ___ ___ ___ ___ ___ ___ ___ (8 20 18 21 26 25 10 23)?

**4** Ana would like to ___ ___ ___ ___ ___ (2 6 25 8 13) a ___ ___ ___ ___ ___ ___ ___ (18 4 24 25 10 23 4) movie.

**5** Would you like to ___ ___ (12 20) to the ___ ___ ___ ___ ___ ___ ___ (25 13 10 6 25 10 23)?

# PROJECT 4

**1** Read the article. Match the headings with the paragraphs.

Opinion   Equipment   Rules   ~~History~~

## JAI ALAI

1 History

Jai Alai is over 300 years old. It comes from the Basque region of Spain. The name means "merry festival" because people played Jai Alai during special festivals. Some people say that Jai Alai is the fastest game in the world because the ball can go faster than 300 km/h.

2 ______________

To play Jai Alai, you need a small, hard ball and a special basket, called a *cesta*. You should also protect your head with a helmet because the ball can be dangerous. Jai Alai players usually wear white pants, a colored shirt, and a red belt.

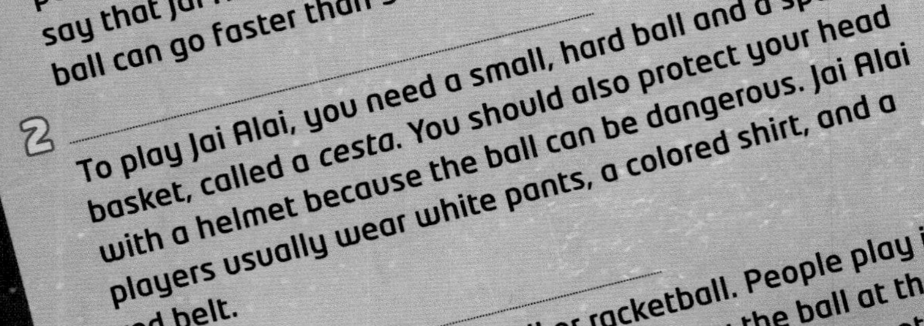

3 ______________

Jai Alai is similar to handball or racketball. People play it on a special court with three walls. You throw the ball at the front wall with your *cesta* and it bounces back. Then the other team has to catch the ball, and throw it again. You can also play Jai Alai in teams, with two or four players on each team.

4 ______________

Jai Alai is popular in many countries. It's fun to play, and it's good exercise, too. It's also an exciting sport for fans to watch because it's very fast. The only problem is that Jai Alai is too expensive for many people. For example, a special Jai Alai ball costs about $150, but it only lasts for about fifteen minutes. I love Jai Alai, and I think more people should play it or watch it.

**2** Choose an interesting sport. Make notes about the sport's history, equipment, and rules. Think about your own opinion, too. Use the headings in exercise 1.

**3** Write your sports profile on a poster. Use the model to help you. Find photos or draw pictures to decorate your poster.

**4** Present your sports profile poster to the class.

Alistair McCallum   Claire Thacker

# engage

2nd edition

# Welcome

## Vocabulary

### Weather

**1** Write the weather words.

1 It's sunny.

2 It's ________.

3 It's ________.

4 It's ________.

5 It's ________.

6 It's ________.

### Clothes

**2** Find eight clothes words in the wordsearch.

| S | H | O | E | S | A | Q | P | I | E | P | F |
|---|---|---|---|---|---|---|---|---|---|---|---|
| H | C | I | P | O | Z | N | G | Y | N | A | O |
| I | A | K | S | C | G | R | M | J | F | N | B |
| R | B | F | J | K | P | S | K | I | R | T | O |
| T | E | U | T | S | B | D | R | L | Q | S | O |
| D | C | O | L | V | H | W | T | O | P | R | T |
| G | L | A | S | S | E | S | M | H | K | X | S |

### Physical descriptions

**3** Write the words. Find the hidden description.

| | | | | | | | |
|---|---|---|---|---|---|---|---|
| | | 1 B | L | O | N | D | |
| 2 | | | | | | | |
| | 3 | | | | | | |
| 4 | | | | | | | |
| | | 5 | | | | | |

### Possessions

**4** Unscramble the possessions.

1 l e b t — b e l t
2 e y k — ___ ___ ___
3 c a p k a c b k — ___ ___ ___ ___ ___ ___ ___ ___
4 n e k g r i y — ___ ___ ___ ___ ___ ___ ___
5 g r i s e r a n — ___ ___ ___ ___ ___ ___ ___ ___
6 l a b e r t c e — ___ ___ ___ ___ ___ ___ ___ ___

## Food and drink

**1 Fill in the blanks with the correct food and drink words.**

1 I'm having a  hamburger________ and  ____________ for dinner.

2 Do you want some  ____________?

3 Let's have ____________ and  ____________ for lunch.

4 My brother doesn't like  ____________.

5 My parents always drink  ____________ in the morning.

6 My favorite fruit is  ____________.

## Jobs

**2 Fill in the blanks with vowels.**

1 a rt i st
2 ___rch___t___ct
3 wr___t___r
4 ___nv___nt___r
5 p___l___t___c___n
6 sc______nt___st

## Music

**3 Unscramble the letters. Then fill in the blanks.**

1 My favorite kind of music is pop________. **opp**
2 Do you like ____________ music? **zjaz**
3 Sandra loves ____________ music. **ckor**
4 My friends are in a ____________ group. **arp**
5 We sometimes listen to ____________ music in the car. **tonruyc**
6 I don't like ____________ music, but my parents love it! **liscalacs**

## Musical instruments

**4 Find eight musical instruments in the wordsearch.**

| T | R | U | M | P | E | T | D | A | F | C | K |
|---|---|---|---|---|---|---|---|---|---|---|---|
| W | N | G | U | I | T | A | R | O | X | I | E |
| I | S | A | T | A | R | T | U | H | V | N | Y |
| D | J | M | D | N | U | F | M | B | I | K | B |
| E | Q | O | U | O | L | H | S | P | O | G | O |
| K | Z | E | L | K | B | M | C | P | L | H | A |
| S | A | X | O | P | H | O | N | E | I | Y | R |
| V | R | B | A | S | S | G | Q | J | N | S | D |

## Nature

**5 Write the nature words.**

1 beach________ 2 ____________

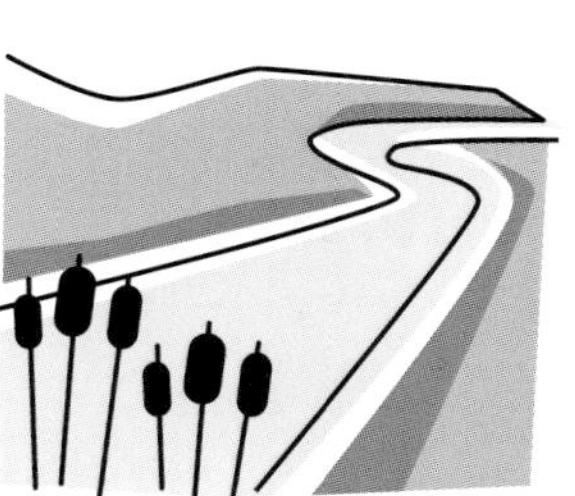

3 ____________ 4 ____________

5 ____________ 6 ____________

# Grammar

## Present progressive (affirmative and negative)

**1** **Circle the correct form.**

1 I **'s** / **'m** drinking some soda right now.
2 He **'s** / **'m** babysitting his sister now.
3 We **aren't** / **isn't** watching TV.
4 You **aren't** / **isn't** doing your homework at the moment.
5 She **aren't** / **isn't** sending a text message now.
6 They **is** / **are** wearing blue shirts today.

**2** **Complete the sentences with the affirmative or negative form of the verbs in parentheses. Use the present progressive.**

1 We *'re swimming* in the ocean. It's great! (✓ swim)
2 They ………… near the river. (✗ sit)
3 She ………… a meal. (✓ cook)
4 I ………… a comment on your web page. (✗ post)
5 You ………… to me! (✗ listen)
6 He ………… in the yard at the moment. (✓ work)

## Present progressive (questions)

**3** **Fill in the blanks with the present progressive form of the verbs.**

**buy**
A: What (1) *are* you (2) *buying* ?
B: I (3) *'m buying* a book.

**wait**
A: Where (4) ………… they (5) ………… ?
B: They (6) ………… at the bus stop.

**go**
A: Where (7) ………… you (8) ………… ?
B: We (9) ………… to the bowling alley.

**do / climb**
A: What (10) ………… you (11) ………… ?
B: I (12) ………… a mountain!

**do / chat**
A: What (13) ………… he (14) ………… ?
B: He (15) ………… online.

## Present progressive and simple present

**4** **Circle the correct form.**

1 I **play** / **'m playing** the guitar right now.
2 It **rains** / **'s raining** today.
3 My best friends **aren't liking** / **don't like** country music.
4 She **uses** / **is using** a red backpack today.
5 You **eat** / **are eating** strawberries for breakfast every day.
6 It's sunny today. We **wear** / **'re wearing** sunglasses.

## *a / an / some / any* (countable nouns)

**5** **Complete the sentences with *a*, *an*, *some*, or *any*.**

1 There's *an* apple on your desk.
2 Are there ………… bananas?
3 There isn't ………… pear in the refrigerator.
4 There aren't ………… tomatoes for the salad.
5 Is there ………… egg for me?
6 There are ………… mangoes over there.

## Countable and uncountable nouns

**6** **Circle C (countable) or U (uncountable).**

1 belt C / U
2 cheese C / U
3 coffee C / U
4 rice C / U
5 soda C / U
6 egg C / U
7 potato C / U
8 salt C / U
9 shirt C / U
10 key C / U

## *How much / many* + quantifiers

**1** **Look at the picture. Complete the questions and answers with *much, many, a lot, a few, any,* or *none*.**

1 How much ............ ketchup is there?
There's a little ............ ketchup.
2 How ............ salad is there?
There's ............ of salad.
3 How ............ tomatoes are there?
There are ............ tomatoes.
4 How ............ eggs are there?
There are ............ of eggs.
5 How ............ juice is there?
There isn't ............ juice.
6 How ............ potatoes are there?
There are ............ .

## Possessive adjectives and pronouns

**2** **Circle the correct word.**

1 **A:** Whose backpack is that?
**B:** It's **my** / **mine**.
2 **A:** Is this your cell phone?
**B:** No, it's **he** / **his**.
3 **A:** Hey! Those aren't **your** / **yours** sneakers.
**B:** Oh, sorry!
4 **A:** Whose DVDs are these?
**B:** They're **our** / **ours**.
5 **A:** Are these your shoes?
**B:** No. They're **her** / **hers**.
6 **A:** Whose belt is this?
**B:** It's **you** / **yours**!

## *can / can't* (permission)

**3** **Fill in the blanks with the verbs below.**

borrow ~~buy~~ come go have stay out

1 Mom, can we please buy ............ a dog?
2 Can I ............ a new bike for my birthday, please?
3 Can we ............ until midnight tonight?
4 Can my friend ............ to our house on the weekend?
5 Can we ............ to Maria's party?
6 Can I ............ your cell phone, please?

## Suggestions

**4** **Choose the correct words.**

1 **Let's** / **What about** go to the library.
2 Why don't we **have** / **having** a party?
3 What about **to watch** / **watching** a movie later?
4 Let's **go** / **going** to the amusement park.
5 **Let's** / **What about** playing soccer in the park?
6 Let's **have** / **having** a party after school today.

## *was / were*

**5** **Fill in the blanks with *was* or *were*. Then write short answers.**

1 Were ............ you at the pool yesterday? (✗)
No, I wasn't ............ .
2 ............ Selena in the coffee shop after school? (✓)
............ .
3 ............ your friends in the park last Saturday? (✗)
............ .
4 ............ your brother at the shopping mall yesterday? (✗)
............ .
5 ............ you in the library this morning? (✓)
............ .
6 ............ Ellie and Kate at the museum last weekend? (✓)
............ .

## Simple past: affirmative (regular and irregular)

**1 Write the simple past form of the verbs. Then decide if they are R (regular) or I (irregular).**

1 chat *chatted* ........ *R*
2 babysit ........ ....
3 stay ........ ....
4 try ........ ....
5 make ........ ....
6 swim ........ ....
7 send ........ ....
8 climb ........ ....
9 like ........ ....
10 ride ........ ....
11 drink ........ ....
12 move ........ ....

**2 Complete the sentences with the simple past affirmative form of the verbs in parentheses.**

1 Our team *won* ........ the soccer game yesterday! (win)
2 We ........ a funny show on TV last night. (watch)
3 Gilberto ........ to Chile last year. (move)
4 I ........ in a river on vacation last summer. (swim)
5 You ........ your sister's boots. (borrow)
6 Li-mi ........ a delicious cake for her mother. (make)

## Simple past: negative

**3 Check (✓) the correct sentence.**

1 a Barack Obama didn't win the Nobel Prize in 2011. ✓
  b Barack Obama didn't won the Nobel Prize in 2011.
2 a Alicia Keys didn't sang a song with Shakira.
  b Alicia Keys didn't sing a song with Shakira.
3 a The Aztecs didn't build the Pyramids.
  b The Aztecs didn't built the Pyramids.
4 a Johnny Depp didn't act in *Transformers*.
  b Johnny Depp acted not in *Transformers*.
5 a Pelé didn't to play in the 2010 World Cup.
  b Pelé didn't play in the 2010 World Cup.
6 a The *Titanic* didn't sink in 1900.
  b The *Titanic* didn't sank in 1900.

## Simple past: questions

**4 What did they do yesterday? Write the simple past questions. Then answer them.**

1 Silvia / buy / DVDs
*Did Silvia buy DVDs* ........?
*Yes, she did* .
2 Jin-woo / play / basketball
........?
........ .
3 Silvia and Jin-woo / go to Boston
........?
........ .
4 Silvia and Jin-woo / see a rock concert
........?
........ .
5 Silvia / eat a hamburger
........?
........ .
6 Jin-woo / buy a soccer magazine
........?
........ .

 Student Book p.10

# 1 My time

## Grammar reference

### Gerunds (*-ing* form)

| *like / enjoy / love / don't like / hate* + *-ing* form | | |
|---|---|---|
| I / You / We / They | **love**<br>**don't like** | play**ing** tennis. |
| He / She / It | **enjoys**<br>**doesn't like** | read**ing** magazines. |

We use gerunds when we talk about personal likes and dislikes.
Sarah doesn't like playing soccer. She loves painting.
We use *do / does* + *not* to make gerunds negative.
James and Liz don't like shopping.

### *-ing* form + *be* + adjective

| *-ing* form + *be* + adjective | |
|---|---|
| Running | **is boring**. |
| Doing karate | **is interesting**. |

We use the *-ing* form to change verbs to nouns in a sentence. We can use *-ing* + *be* + adjective to describe how we feel about those things.
Shopping in the mall is boring.

### *have to*

| Affirmative | Negative |
|---|---|
| **Obligation** | **No obligation** |
| I / You **have to** set the table. | I / You **don't have to** wash the dishes. |
| He / She / It **has to** cut the grass. | He / She / It **doesn't have to** make lunch. |
| You / We / They **have to** wash the dishes. | You / We / They **don't have to** set the table. |
| **Questions** | **Short answers** |
| **Do** you **have to** do chores? | Yes, I **do**. / No, I **don't**. |
| **Does** he / she **have to** do chores? | Yes, he / she **does**. / No, he / she **doesn't**. |

We use the affirmative of *have to* for talking about obligations.
I have to take out the garbage.
We use the negative of *have to* for talking about things that are not obligations.
He doesn't have to make his bed.

## Word list

### Leisure activities

doing karate
listening to music
painting
playing soccer
playing the guitar
reading magazines
shopping
using the computer

### Chores at home

clean (your) room
cut the grass
make lunch
make (your) bed
put away (your) clothes
set the table
take out the garbage
wash the dishes

# Vocabulary

**1** **Complete the puzzle with the leisure activities.**

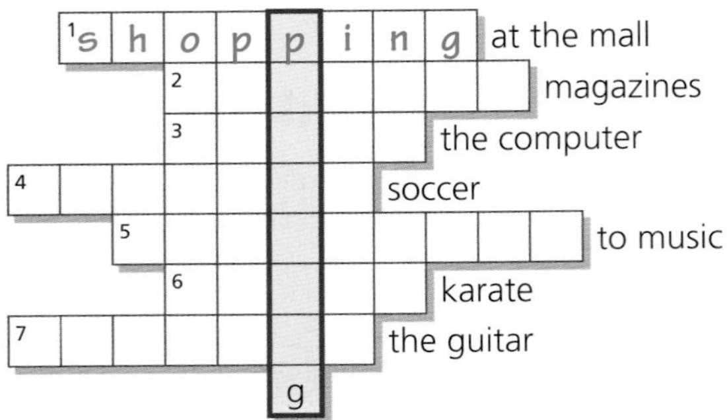


**What's the mystery word?** ..............................

**2** **Look at the pictures. Circle the correct adjective.**

1 Swimming is **fun** / **awful**.
2 It's **awful** / **fun**.
3 Watching TV is **boring** / **great**.
4 No, it isn't. It's **boring** / **great**.
5 Playing games is **OK** / **exciting**.
6 It's **fun** / **OK**!
7 Painting pictures is **fun** / **OK**.
8 No, it isn't. It's **fun** / **boring**.

## Extend your vocabulary

**3** **Fill in the blankswith the correct form of the words below.**

~~acting~~ camping having a barbecue hiking rock climbing skateboarding

1 Acting .............................. is fun!

2 We love .............................. !

3 We like .............................. .

4 .............................. is fun!

5 .............................. is cool!

6 .............................. is great!


Student Book p.11

# Grammar

**1 Write the *-ing* form of the verbs.**

1 go → going
2 sit → ...........
3 practice → ...........
4 read → ...........
5 run → ...........
6 give → ...........
7 look → ...........
8 live → ...........

**2 Circle the correct word.**

1 My brother **enjoy** / **enjoys** singing.
2 **Play** / **Playing** soccer is fun.
3 **Do** / **Does** you enjoy painting?
4 My friends **do** / **don't** like shopping.
5 I love **read** / **reading** computer magazines.
6 **Do** / **Does** your mom like watching TV?

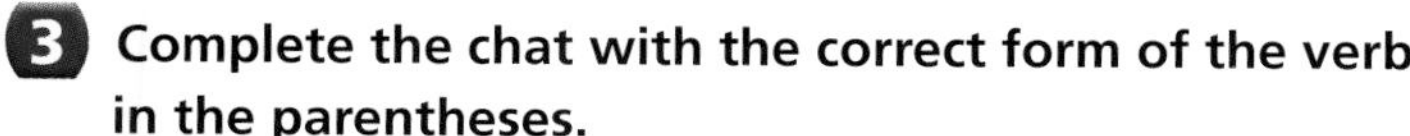

**3 Complete the chat with the correct form of the verbs in the parentheses.**

**Rick says:** Hi, Eva. Do you like books?

**Eva says:** Hello, Ricky. Yes, I [1] love reading (love / read)! And I like watching movies.

**Ricky says:** Me too. [2] ........... (go / to the movies) is fun. And I like watching TV.

**Eva says:** [3] ........... (watch / TV) is OK. I like music, too. I [4] ........... (like / play) the violin, but I'm not very good.

**Ricky says:** Wow! The violin! I don't play an instrument, but I [5] ........... (enjoy / listen) to music.

**Eva says:** My dad's a musician. He [6] ........... (love / play) with his band. He plays the saxophone.

**Ricky says:** That's amazing! [7] ........... (play / the saxophone) is really difficult!

**Eva says:** Yes, I know. He practices every evening. Mom [8] ........... (hate / listen) to him practice!

1

# Vocabulary

**1 Label the pictures with words from the word snake.**

clothesgrassdishesmakegarbagecleanlunchtakeouttablemakeroomcutbedsetwashputaway

1 make my bed

2 ________ ________

3 ________ ________ the ________

4 ________ my ________

5 ________ the ________

6 ________ the ________

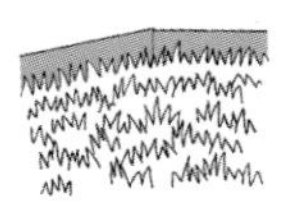
7 ________ the ________

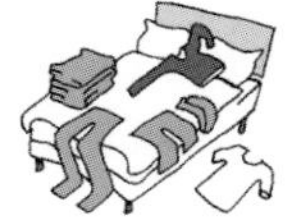
8 ________ ________ my ________

**2 Correct the verbs.**

1 I have to ~~set~~ the garbage.
take out

2 My brother has to clean the grass.
________

3 I have to take out my clothes every day.
________

4 Do you have to wash the table for dinner?
________

5 My mother doesn't have to take out lunch.
________

6 We have to make our rooms.
________

**Extend your vocabulary**

**3 Label the pictures with the verbs below.**

do dust ~~fix~~ polish sweep unload

1 fix the car

2 ________ the floor

3 ________ the dishwasher

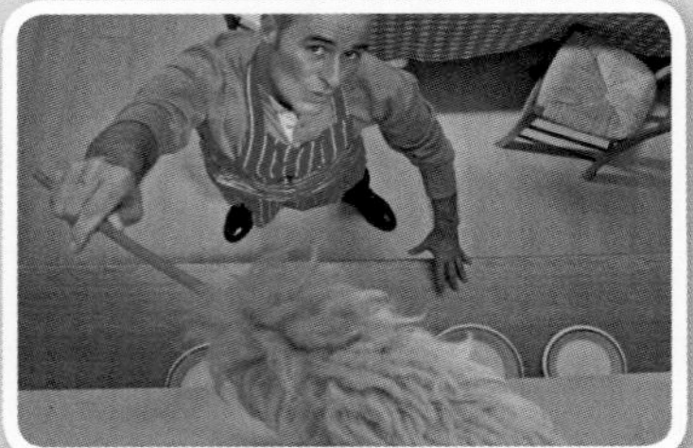
4 ________ the furniture

5 ________ the laundry

6 ________ your boots

## Grammar

| Chores for the weekend | | | | |
|---|---|---|---|---|
| | Tom | Tilly | Mom | Dad |
| cut the grass | | ✓ | ✓ | |
| wash the dishes | | ✓ | | ✓ |
| make lunch | ✓ | ✓ | | ✓ |
| fix the car | | | | ✓ |
| do the laundry | ✓ | ✓ | | |
| make the beds | | | ✓ | ✓ |

**1** **Look at the chart. Circle the correct form of the verb.**

1 Mom **doesn't have to** / **has to** cut the grass.
2 Tom and Tilly **don't have to** / **have to** make their beds.
3 Mom **has to** / **doesn't have to** fix the car.
4 Tilly and Dad **have to** / **don't have to** wash the dishes.
5 **Do** / **Does** Tilly have to do the laundry?

**2** **Look at the chart again. Match the sentences with the people.**

1 "We have to do the laundry."
2 "I don't have to make lunch."
3 "I have to fix the car."
4 "We don't have to wash the dishes."
5 "I have to wash the dishes, but I don't have to make the beds."

a Dad
b Tom and Mom
c Tilly
d Tilly and Tom
e Mom

**3** **Read Tom's e-mail to his friend. Fill in the blanks with *have to, has to, don't have to,* or *doesn't have to.***

Hi Jerry,

There's a lot to do this weekend! The car isn't working, so Dad (1) has to ________ fix it. Tilly and I (2) ________ do the laundry, but we (3) ________ make our beds. Mom (4) ________ cut the grass, because it's too long. Mom usually has to make lunch, but she (5) ________ make lunch this weekend. Tilly and Dad (6) ________ wash the dishes. I (7) ________ wash the dishes, but I (8) ________ make lunch with Tilly. Do you have to do any chores on the weekends?

See you soon,

Tom

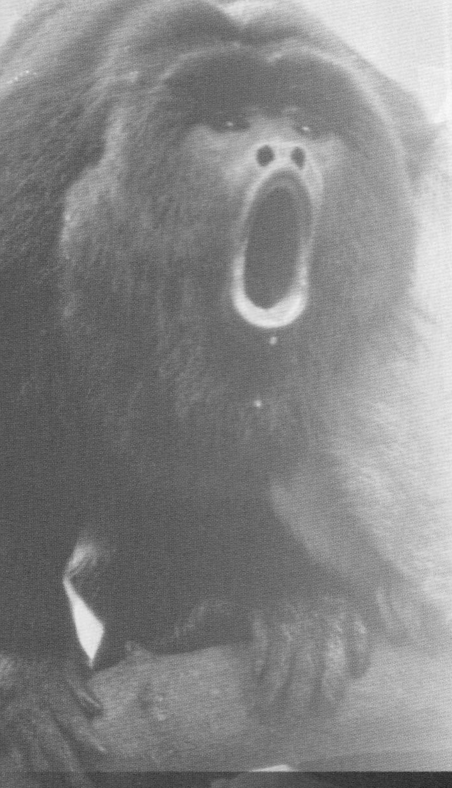

# Come and volunteer today!

### 1 The project

The black howler monkey lives in the rainforests in the south of Brazil, the north of Argentina, Paraguay, and Bolivia. But it is in danger because those rainforests are disappearing. Can you help? Come and work with us at our black howler monkey rescue center in Brazil. You have to pay for your trip, and working with us for three weeks costs $670.

### 2 What do I have to do?

Volunteers have to love animals. You have to be patient, and you have to be in good shape because we do a lot of walking and carrying heavy plates of food. You don't work alone, and you have to share a bedroom with two or three other people. And one more thing: you don't have to speak Spanish, but it helps!

### 3 The daily routine

You have to work every day from 9 a.m. until 8 p.m. It isn't easy, but it's good fun. Every day you have to prepare the monkeys' food and feed them. After that, you have to wash the dishes. Then you have to look after and play with the monkeys. You also have to clean your bedroom and the toilets. Finally, you have to help look after the other animals, too: lions, cats, sheep, ducks, and chickens.

**Why not check out our website now and come and join us?**

## Reading

**1 Read the advertisement quickly. Answer the questions.**

1 Where is the project? Brazil
2 Is it a difficult job? ……
3 Do you have to like animals? ……

**2 Read again. Complete the sentences with *have to* or *don't have to*.**

1 You have to …… do a lot of walking.
2 You …… work on your own.
3 You …… clean your bedroom.
4 You …… work after 8 p.m.
5 You …… speak Spanish.
6 You …… look after other animals.

**3 Correct the sentences.**

1 Black howler monkeys live in Chile.
Black howler monkeys live in southern Brazil, northern Argentina, Paraguay, and Bolivia.
2 You have your own bedroom.
……
3 You start work every day at 8 a.m.
……
4 You don't have to work on the weekends.
……
5 It's free to travel to the rescue center.
……
6 You only have to look after the howler monkeys.
……

# 2 Get moving!

## Grammar reference

### *can / can't* (rules)

| Affirmative | |
|---|---|
| I / You / We / They **can park** here.<br>He / She / It **can park** here. | |
| **Negative** | |
| I / You / We / They **can't park** here.<br>He / She / It **can park** here. | |
| **Questions** | **Short answers** |
| **Can** we **park** here? | Yes, you **can**. / No, you **can't**. |

We use *can* to talk about rules and to explain that something is or is not allowed.
You can play soccer here.
You can't swim in this part of the ocean.
The form of *can / can't* is the same for all persons.
I can't leave my bike here.
You can't leave your bike here.
He / She can't leave his / her bike here.
They can't leave their bikes here.
We use *can* + subject + infinitive without *to* to form questions.
Can I take photos in the museum?

### *too / not … enough*

| *too* + adjective | *not* + adjective + enough |
|---|---|
| It's **too** dangerous. | It is**n't** safe **enough**. |

We form *too* sentences with *too* + adjective.
You're too young to watch this movie.
We form *not … enough* sentences with *not* + adjective + *enough*.
You aren't old enough to watch this movie.

## Word list

### Transportation

airplane
bus
canoe
car
ferry
helicopter
motorcycle
sailboat
subway
train

### Opposite adjectives

comfortable
dangerous
difficult
easy
fast
quiet
noisy
safe
slow
uncomfortable

2

## Vocabulary

**1 Label the pictures of different kinds of transportation.**

1 bus

2

3

4

5

6

**2 Complete the crossword.**

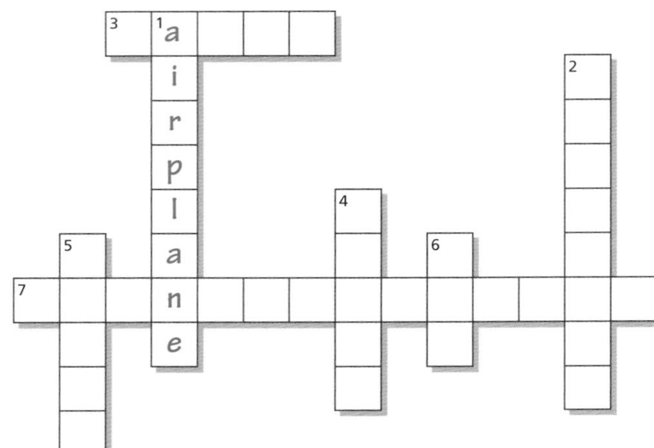


1 We're flying to Vermont next summer. We're going by airplane .
2 My uncle goes sailing in his ______ every weekend.
3 I traveled on a river in a ______ on a school trip. It was awesome!
4 You can take a ______ to travel across the river.
5 My dad takes the ______ to work every day from Grand Central station.
6 Do your parents drive you to school by ______?
7 There are many kinds of ______.

Extend your vocabulary

**3 Fill in the blanks with the words below.**

cruise ship hot air balloon scooter taxi ~~trolley~~ truck

1 I love taking the trolley in San Francisco.

2 We took a yellow ______ in New York.

3 Look at that beautiful ______.

4 My grandparents took a ______ to Barbados.

5 Joe's dad drives a ______ for his job.

6 My brother got a ______ for his sixteenth birthday.

 Student Book p.19

## Grammar

**1** **Circle the correct word.**

1 You **can** / **can't** drive my car. You don't have a driver's license.
2 We usually wear school uniform, but today we **can** / **can't** wear jeans to school.
3 Kenji **can** / **can't** come to the soccer game. He doesn't have a ticket.
4 You **can** / **can't** touch the ball with your hand in soccer.
5 I **can** / **can't** leave school today at twelve o'clock. This afternoon is a holiday.
6 This is a no-parking zone. You **can** / **can't** park your car here.

**2** **Complete the sentences with *can* or *can't*.**

1 You can't swim here.

2 You ............ cycle here.

3 You ............ go online here.

4 You ............ play soccer here.

5 You ............ take photos here.

6 You ............ use your cell phone here.

**3** **Look at the school rules. Write sentences with *can* or *can't*.**

SCHOOL RULES

chew gum in class ✗
use cell phones during class ✗
use calculators ✓
run in the hallways ✗
use cell phones between classes ✓
eat in the cafeteria or outside ✓

1 You can't chew gum in class.
2 ............
3 ............
4 ............
5 ............
6 ............

2

## Vocabulary

**1 Fill in the blanks to complete the adjectives. Then write the opposite adjectives.**

1 f*a*st → *slow*
2 q___t → ______
3 c_mf_rt_bl_ → ______
4 d_ng_r_s → ______
5 d_ff_c_lt → ______

**2 Fill in the blanks with adjectives from exercise 1.**

1 The train home is very *slow*. It stops everywhere.
2 Our homework was very ______. I finished it in fifteen minutes!
3 Traveling by airplane is very ______, but a lot of people are scared.
4 The library is a ______ place. You can't talk here.
5 Sitting on the bus for a long time is ______.
6 That highway is ______. There are a lot of accidents, and too many fast cars.

**Extend your vocabulary**

**3 Label the pictures with the words below.**

cheap exciting expensive ~~new~~ old scary

1 *new*

2 ______

3 ______

4 ______

5 ______

6 ______

## Grammar

**1 Circle the correct words.**

1 I don't understand this book. It's too difficult / not difficult enough.
2 Tim's only fourteen years old. He can't drive a car. He **'s too old / isn't old enough**.
3 We can't go out in our sailboat today. The ocean is **too dangerous / not dangerous enough**.
4 They went to the park to talk because café the was **too quiet / not quiet enough**.
5 You can't buy that DVD. You have to be eighteen to watch it. You **'re too old / aren't old enough**.
6 We can't go on foot to the shopping mall. It **'s too close / isn't close enough**.

**2 Fill in the blanks with *too* and the adjectives below.**

dangerous expensive ~~hot~~ loud

1 We can't go out in the sun now. It's 40°C. It's too hot ______.
2 I like that car, but it's $500,000. That's ______!
3 Don't swim across that river. There are crocodiles! It's ______.
4 Sorry, I can't hear you. The music here is ______.

**3 Fill in the blanks with *not … enough* and the adjectives below.**

big comfortable old ~~warm~~

1 I don't want to go to the beach today. It is n't warm enough ______.
2 We can't put all these suitcases in the car. It is ______.
3 I can't sit here. It is ______.
4 I want to get a driver's license, but I'm only fifteen. I'm ______.

**4 These people can't be lifeguards. Why not? Write sentences about the people using *too* or *not … enough*, and the words in parentheses.**

1 Sally is 1.55 m tall. (tall) She isn't tall enough ______.
2 Jack is 59. (old) ______.
3 Lucy weighs 55 kg. (heavy) ______.
4 Sam is fourteen. (old) ______.
5 Dom weighs 95 kg. (heavy) ______.
6 Tony can swim 3 km/h. (fast) ______.

Abby Sunderland is a sixteen-year-old sailor from California. She went on her first sailboat when she was six months old, and she has a lot of experience. But was she too young to sail around the world alone? On January 23rd, 2010, Abby began a round-the-world trip. She left Marina Del Rey, California in her sailboat "Wild Eyes", but her journey ended on June 10th in the Indian Ocean. The weather wasn't good enough for the trip because it was winter. The ocean was too dangerous, and the winds were too strong. Part of her sailboat broke.

An Australian airplane saw her 3,200 kilometers from the west coast of Australia. The airplane sent a message to other boats, and a French fishing boat finally found her after 40 hours. Then she traveled by boat for eight hours to Réunion.

When she was on dry land again, she ate breakfast, called her parents, and changed her clothes. Her brother, Zac, met her and they went home together by airplane. Her family was very happy that she was safe again. This was a scary experience, and perhaps Abby wasn't old enough. For now, her round-the-world dream is over.

## Reading

**1 Read the article quickly. Choose the best title.**

a Was it a dangerous sailboat?
b Was she old enough to sail alone?
c Was she too tired to sail?

**2 Circle the correct word.**

1 Abby Sunderland has her own (sailboat) / **airplane**.
2 An Australian **boat / airplane** saw her.
3 A French **boat / airplane** took her to Réunion.
4 Abby and Zac traveled home by **boat / airplane**.

**3 Complete the sentences with *too* or *be + not … enough* and the adjectives in parentheses.**

1 Was she *too young* to sail around the world alone? (young)
2 The weather ______ for her trip. (good)
3 The ocean was ______. (dangerous)
4 The winds were ______. (strong)
5 Abby ______ to do this. (old)

**4 Are the sentences T (True) or F (False)? Correct the false sentences.**

1 Abby Sunderland is from Australia.
T / (F) *Abby isn't from Australia. She's from the U.S.*
2 She began sailing when she was a baby.
T / F ______
3 She began her journey on June 10th, 2010.
T / F ______
4 It took 40 hours to travel to Réunion.
T / F ______
5 The ocean wasn't dangerous enough.
T / F ______

# 3 Crime scene

## Grammar reference

### Past progressive (affirmative / negative)

| Affirmative | Negative |
|---|---|
| I **was talking**. | I **wasn't shouting**. |
| You **were running**. | You **weren't walking**. |
| He / She / It **was hiding**. | He / She / It **wasn't fighting**. |
| We / They **were arguing**. | We / They **weren't talking**. |

We use the past progressive to talk about actions in progress in the past.
I was arguing with my brother.
They were shouting at each other.
We form the past progressive negative with subject + *was* / *were* + *not* + verb *-ing* form.
He wasn't walking.
Alicia and Maria weren't doing their homework.

### Past progressive (questions)

| ***yes* / *no* questions** | **Answers** | |
|---|---|---|
| **Was** I shouting? | Yes, I **was**. | No, I **wasn't**. |
| **Were** you complaining? | Yes, you **were**. | No, you **weren't**. |
| **Was** he / she / it running? | Yes, he / she / it **was**. | No, he / she / it **wasn't**. |
| **Were** we / you / they fighting? | Yes, we / you / they **were**. | No, we / you / they **weren't**. |
| ***Wh-* questions** | **Answers** | |
| Where **was** she going? | She **was** going to the movies. | |
| What **were** they doing? | They **were** doing their homework. | |

We use the past progressive to ask about actions in progress in the past.
Was Pablo singing?
What were Chen and Aya listening to?
We form *yes* / *no* questions with *Was* / *Were* + subject + verb *-ing* form.
Was he eating? Yes, he was.
Were you sending a text message? No, I wasn't.
We form *Wh-* questions with *Wh-* question words + *was* / *were* + subject + verb *-ing* form.
Why were you arguing? Because I wanted to use the computer.
Where was Scott waiting? He was waiting on the street corner.

## Word list

### Conflict verbs

argue
complain
fight
hide
hit
shout

### Places in a street

apartment
bank
fire escape
garage
police station
street corner

# Vocabulary

## 1 Match the pictures with the sentences below.

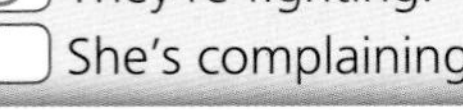
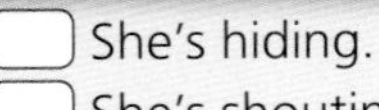
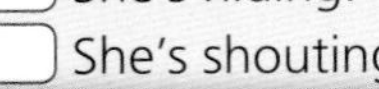
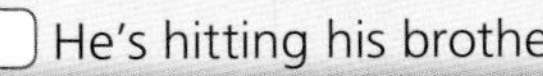

- [5] They're fighting.
- [ ] She's complaining.
- [ ] She's hiding.
- [ ] She's shouting.
- [ ] They're arguing.
- [ ] He's hitting his brother.

## 2 Fill in the blanks with the verbs below.

argue complain fight hide hit ~~shout~~

1 Please don't *shout*. I'm watching TV.
2 We have a cat and a dog, but they never ________.
3 A lot of people ________ about the food in that restaurant. It's terrible.
4 Don't ________ your little sister!
5 Do you often ________ with your friends about things?
6 I can't find Andi. Where did he ________?

**Extend your vocabulary**

## 3 Fill in the blanks with the words below.

judge lawyer police officer ~~robber~~ witness

On Monday, a (1) *robber* stole £100,000 from the Central Bank. The next day, a (2) ________ arrested the robber. In court, a (3) ________ told the (4) ________, "I saw him on Monday. He was running down the street with a bag full of money. He was holding a gun. He stole the money!" The (5) ________ sent the robber to prison for ten years.

## Grammar

**1 Circle the correct word.**

1 Kenta **was** / **were** arguing with Alice at the party.
2 We **wasn't** / **weren't** waiting for a bus at 4 p.m. We **was** / **were** waiting for a taxi.
3 The sun **was** / **were** shining yesterday afternoon.
4 Martha **wasn't** / **weren't** watching a movie at 8 p.m. She **was** / **were** playing a computer game.
5 I **was** / **were** sleeping when you called last night.
6 Eric and Vitor **was** / **were** listening to music yesterday evening.

**2 Look at the chart. Complete the dialogues with the past progressive of the verbs in parentheses.**

| | Ellie | Harry | Serena | Dan |
|---|---|---|---|---|
| 5:30 – 6:30 | dinner | dinner | music | dinner |
| 6:30 – 7:30 | TV | soccer with Abdul | | |
| 7:30 – 8:30 | | | | DVDs with Jenny |
| 8:30 – 9:30 | homework | homework | magazine | homework |

**1** Serena: I (1) *was doing* (do) my homework at 6 p.m. yesterday evening.
Ellie: That's not true! You (2) .................... (not do) your homework.
You (3) .................... (listen) to music!

**2** Ellie: I (4) .................... (watch) TV at 7 p.m. What about you? Were you at home?
Harry: No, I wasn't. I was in the park with Abdul. We (5) .................... (play) soccer.

**3** Dan's dad: Who was in your room at 8 p.m.? It was noisy. Your radio was too loud!
Dan: I was with Jenny. We (6) .................... (not listen) to the radio.
We (7) .................... (watch) DVDs.

**3 These sentences are incorrect. Write the correct sentences.**

1 Ellie was having dinner at 7 p.m.
She *wasn't having dinner*. She *was watching* TV.
2 Dan was sleeping at 9 p.m.
He .................... . He .................... his homework.
3 Serena was watching TV at 9 p.m.
.................... . .................... .
4 Harry and Ellie were doing their homework at 6 p.m.
.................... . .................... .

3

# Vocabulary

**1 Fill in the blanks with the words below.**

apartment   bank   fire escape   garage   police station   ~~street corner~~

1 Where were you? I was waiting on the *street corner*, but I didn't see you!
2 Quick! The building is burning! Run to the ____________!
3 They arrested the robbers and took them to the ____________.
4 You can keep your money in the ____________.
5 When Tony gets home from work, he leaves his car in the ____________.
6 In cities, a lot of people live in an ____________ building.

**2 Correct the mistakes in the sentences.**

1 The car is in the ~~bank~~ today. *garage*
2 I live in a police station. ____________
3 Do you have a lot of money in the garage? ____________
4 Why were you standing on the apartment this morning? ____________
5 You have to use the bank when there is a fire. ____________
6 Someone stole my bike, so I went to the street corner. ____________

## Extend your vocabulary

**3 Label the pictures with the words below.**

apartment building   bus station   library   parking lot   ~~post office~~   stadium

1 *post office*

2 ____________

3 ____________

4 ____________

5 ____________

6 ____________

## Grammar

**1 Match the questions and answers.**

1 "Hi, Frank. I saw you at the party. Were you enjoying it?" d
2 "What were you doing yesterday evening?" ......
3 "Why was Lulu carrying a suitcase?" ......
4 "Were you and Helena walking to the bus station?" ......
5 "Where was Sam going yesterday morning?" ......
6 "Were the children playing computer games?" ......

a "Because she was going to her grandmother's house for the weekend."
b "He was going to the dentist."
c "No, they weren't. They were listening to music."
d "Yes, I was. It was great!"
e "I was watching a DVD with Nicky."
f "No, we weren't. We were walking to the library."

**2 Put the words in order to make questions.**

1 at the party / was / she / What / wearing — What was she wearing at the party?
2 running / Why / this morning / you / were ......?
3 they / Where / going / at lunchtime / were ......?
4 raining / it / Was / yesterday morning ......?
5 on Saturday / soccer / playing / Were / they ......?
6 he / was / doing / at 8 p.m. / What ......?

**3 Look at the picture. Write questions with *Where*, *Why*, or *What*.**

At the party yesterday evening …

1 Fiona was shouting.
Why was she shouting?
Because she was angry.

2 Pam and Dev were watching a movie.
What ...... ...... watching?
They were watching *Iron Man 2*.

3 Jess and Paula were talking.
Where ...... ...... ......?
They were talking in the kitchen.

4 Marco was eating.
...... ...... ...... ......?
He was eating pizza.

5 Maggie and Pedro were dancing.
...... ...... ...... ......?
They were dancing in the garden.

6 Antonia was playing an instrument.
...... ...... ...... ......?
She was playing the guitar.

7 Carlos was sleeping.
...... ...... ...... ......?
Because he was very tired!

# Reading

**1** **Look at the titles and pictures from the newspaper articles. What are the articles about?**

## ROBBERS STEAL PAINTINGS

SÃO PAULO, JUNE 13TH

At midday yesterday, three men paid the $2.45 entrance price for the Pinacoteca do Estado museum. Ten minutes later, the men left the museum with two Picasso paintings in a bag, and two paintings by famous Brazilian painters, Di Cavalcanti and Lasar Segall, in another bag. The men were robbers, and the paintings they stole were worth $612,000.

The men walked out of the museum while a group of school children was waiting to come in. The robbers then got into a car, and a driver drove them away with the paintings. Five police officers were working 100 meters away, but they didn't see or hear anything. When they realized the robbers were driving away, it was too late.

This is the second robbery this year at the museum, but the director of the museum says there isn't a problem with security.

## POLICE FIND PAINTINGS

SÃO PAULO, AUGUST 18TH

Today Brazilian police found the last of the four paintings stolen from the Pinacoteca do Estado museum in June this year. They found the other three paintings earlier this month. Police officers arrested two men and they are questioning the men about the paintings.

**2** **Read the articles. Circle the correct words.**

1 Three men entered the museum at midnight / (midday).
2 The men were police officers / robbers.
3 The men put the paintings into two bags / suitcases.
4 The robbers left in a car / truck.

**3** **Complete the sentences with the past progressive or simple past form of the verbs in parentheses.**

1 Three men *paid* the $2.45 entrance price. (pay)
2 A group of school children ________ ________ to come in. (wait)
3 A driver ________ the robbers away in a car. (drive)
4 Five police officers ________ 100 meters away. (work)
5 The police ________ the paintings two months after the robbery. (find)
6 The police ________ two men. (arrest)

**4** **Are the sentences T (True) or F (False)? Correct the false sentences.**

1 The robbery took 30 minutes.
T / (F) *The robbery took ten minutes*.
2 The men stole four paintings.
T / F ________.
3 The robbers ran out of the museum with the paintings.
T / F ________.
4 The museum director is happy with the museum security.
T / F ________.
5 The police found all the stolen paintings at the same time.
T / F ________.
6 The police arrested two men and a woman.
T / F ________.

## Grammar reference

### Past progressive and simple past (*when*)

| Past progressive | Simple past |
|---|---|
| I **was walking** home. | I **saw** my friend David. |
| You **were camping**. | It **started** to rain. |
| He **wasn't studying**. | His father **came** home. |
| They **weren't listening**. | The teacher **asked** a question. |

We use the past progressive to talk about actions in progress in the past.
He was climbing a mountain.
We use the simple past to talk about completed actions in the past.
She saw a shark in the water.

We use the past progressive and simple past with *when* to talk about a completed action that interrupted a longer action taking place in the past.
I was walking down the street when I saw my brother's girlfriend.
Damon and Sheila were watching TV when Marley arrived.

### Adverbs of manner

| Regular adverbs | | |
|---|---|---|
| **Adjective** | **Adverb** | **Example** |
| loud | loud**ly** | They were talking **loudly**. |
| happy | happi**ly** | She was smiling **happily**. |
| careful | careful**ly** | He drove **carefully**. |
| **Irregular adverbs** | | |
| good | **well** | They reacted very **well**. |
| hard | **hard** | She kicked him **hard**. |
| fast | **fast** | I jumped up **fast**. |

We use adverbs of manner to talk about how we do things.
He's driving carefully.
I walked slowly to the bus stop.
We form most regular adverbs by adding *-ly* to the adjective.
The band played loudly.
If an adjective ends with *-y*, the adverb ends with *-ily*.
She was sitting happily on the bus.
Some adverbs are irregular and don't end with *-ly*.
Laura was dancing well.

## Word list

### Natural disasters

blizzard
drought
earthquake
flood
forest fire
hurricane
tornado
tsunami

### Adverbs of manner

angrily
badly
carefully
happily
hard
loudly
politely
well

# Vocabulary

**1** **Unscramble the words and complete the crossword.**

1 uhdogrt
2 zibalzdr
3 ireurchan
4 stofer efir
5 imustan
6 equarhaket
7 dorotan
8 fodol

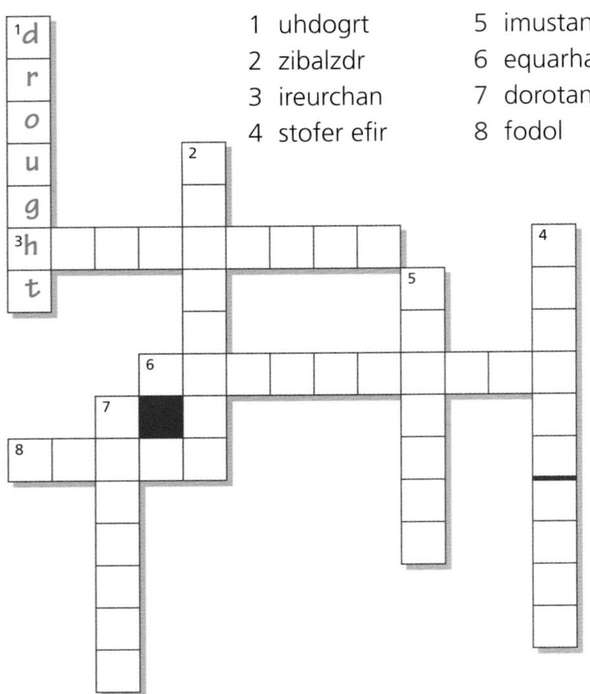


**2** **Complete the newspaper headlines with natural disaster words.**

1 **Huge** tsunami **in the Indian Ocean**
10-meter-high waves hit beaches

2 **A huge ........................ hits New Zealand**
Buildings collapse

3 **........................ Earl hits Bahama Islands**
Winds of 110 km/h

4 **Washington, D.C. hit by ........................**
Snow everywhere

5 **........................ warning in Southern California**
Heavy rain in the region

6 **Huge ........................ hits Kenya**
No rain for six months

Extend your vocabulary

**3** **Label the pictures with the verbs below.**

clean up ~~collapse~~ dig rebuild rescue search for a person

1 collapse

2 ........................

3 ........................

4 ........................

5 ........................

6 ........................

## Grammar

**1 Are these sentences about actions in progress or completed actions? Write P (action in progress) or C (completed action).**

1 Mai dropped a glass. C
2 The children were sleeping. ......
3 I was walking to school. ......
4 Tommy heard a loud noise. ......
5 Yuki passed her exam. ......
6 We were watching TV yesterday evening. ......
7 Marisa bought a new cell phone. ......
8 Mico was practicing the piano. ......

**2 Circle the correct word.**

1 Kana **was** / **were** talking on the phone.
2 My parents were **cook** / **cooking** a meal.
3 I **opened** / **opening** the box, but it was empty.
4 Olga and Karen **wasn't** / **weren't** enjoying the party.
5 Ryo **doesn't** / **didn't** buy the laptop. It was too expensive.
6 Luis **wasn't** / **weren't** running very fast.

**3 These sentences are wrong. Look at the pictures and write correct sentences.**

1 Vincent and Tara were playing soccer.

They weren't playing soccer. They were playing ...... tennis.

2 Sabine broke her leg.

She didn't ...... her leg. She ...... her arm.

3 Mark's parents bought a new house.

They didn't ...... . They ...... car.

4 Paolo was waiting outside the movie theater.

He wasn't ...... . ...... the café.

5 Joe and Millie were eating candy.

They ...... . ...... ice cream.

6 Cassie sent a text message.

...... . ...... an e-mail.

# Vocabulary

**1** **Circle the eight adverbs in the wordsearch. Then write the words.**

| | | | | | | | | |
|---|---|---|---|---|---|---|---|---|
| P | O | L | I | T | E | L | Y | S |
| E | J | H | Z | O | Y | N | S | R |
| Q | S | P | G | D | T | Y | X | B |
| P | T | W | T | H | A | R | D | A |
| A | N | G | R | I | L | Y | W | D |
| S | L | U | X | K | O | B | E | L |
| C | A | R | E | F | U | L | L | Y |
| N | C | L | O | E | D | I | L | N |
| H | A | P | P | I | L | Y | U | N |
| I | V | T | E | S | Y | K | D | E |

1 a ngrily
2 b ..........
3 w ..........
4 h ..........
5 c ..........
6 h ..........
7 l ..........
8 p ..........

**2** **Circle the correct adverb.**

1 You should ride your bike **carefully** / **loudly** in the street.
2 I have to work **angrily** / **hard** for my exams.
3 The children played **happily** / **hard** while their mother was cooking dinner.
4 The soccer team played very **politely** / **well**, and won the game.
5 My dad shouted at me **angrily** / **happily** because I came home late.
6 Lucia **politely** / **badly** asked the teacher to open the window.

**Extend your vocabulary**

**3** **Fill in the blanks with the words below.**

broken ~~funny~~ serious strange tasty valuable

1 We love this comedy show. It's really funny !

2 I can't use this chair. It's .......... !

3 Look at this picture. It's very .......... !

4 Mmm! This food is very .......... .

5 This was my grandmother's ring. It's very .......... .

6 There was an accident near my house yesterday. It was .......... .

 Student Book p.40 

## Grammar

**1 Write the adverbs from these adjectives.**

1 busy → busily
2 beautiful → ____
3 quick → ____
4 lazy → ____
5 strange → ____
6 easy → ____

**2 Circle the correct word.**

1 The students were studying **quiet** / **quietly**.
2 Mr. Davis is a **good** / **well** teacher.
3 Terry is always **happy** / **happily**.
4 We were listening **careful** / **carefully**.
5 Dan doesn't like **loud** / **loudly** music.
6 I play the guitar very **bad** / **badly**!
7 My suitcase is **heavy** / **heavily**.
8 The crowd was shouting **angry** / **angrily**.

**3 Write sentences with adverbs.**

1 She's a slow walker. She walks slowly.
2 They're hard workers. They ____.
3 He's a bad swimmer. He ____.
4 They're good players. They ____.
5 We're quick learners. We ____.

**4 Complete the sentences with adverbs. Use the adjectives in parentheses to form each adverb.**

I was sailing a boat in Tahiti when I heard news about a storm on the radio.
I (1) quickly (quick) called the rescue team,
but the radio didn't work (2) ____ (good).
The storm was coming, so I sailed (3) ____ (careful).
I saw another boat passing by, so I shouted (4) ____ (loud).
They didn't see me. Then I fell over and hit my head (5) ____ (hard).
I woke up 27 hours later and got up (6) ____ (slow) because I felt weak.
After 42 days I got to the coast, and I survived.

# THE 33 SURVIVORS

On August 5th, 2010, 33 Chilean miners went to work in the San José mine, in the Atacama Desert in Chile. On October 14th, 2010, 69 days later, the last miner came home from work.

The miners were working hard in a mine 700 meters underground when part of the mine collapsed. The miners only had a little fish, a few cookies, and a little milk to eat and drink.

Above the miners, rescuers were working quickly to find them. They were digging and listening carefully. After seventeen days, the rescuers contacted the miners. After that, Chile and the world waited. Food started to arrive for the miners through a special hole. They talked to their families for the first time.

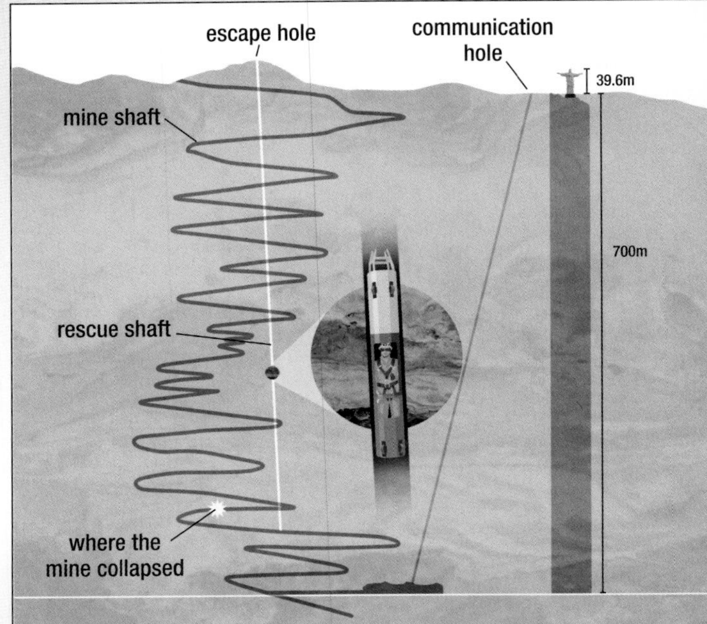


Machines with special equipment began to dig an escape hole at the end of August. The rescue team rescued the first miner safely on October 13th, and the rescue ended happily 22 hours and 37 minutes later.

The miners are now all doing different things. Some are spending more time with their families. One of the miners is enjoying spending time with his new baby daughter; others are exercising more and running marathons. They are all just happy to be alive.

## Reading

**1 Read the text quickly. Answer the questions.**

1 Where is the San José mine? ..................

..................

2 How many days were the miners in the mine?

..................

3 When did the rescue teams rescue the first miner? ..................

**2 Circle the correct adverb.**

1 The miners were working **hard** / **politely** in the mine.
2 The rescuers were working **quickly** / **angrily** to find them.
3 The rescuers were listening **badly** / **carefully**.
4 Rescue teams rescued the first miner **safely** / **quietly**.
5 The rescue ended **happily** / **quietly**.

**3 Complete the summary with the words below.**

collapsed contacted digging escaped equipment ~~miners~~ rescue survive underground

In August 2010, 33 (1) *miners* were working in the San José mine when it (2) .................. . They were working 700 m (3) .................. and they didn't have much food.

After seventeen days, the miners (4) .................. the rescue team who were (5) .................. quickly to find them. The (6) .................. team used special (7) .................. to dig a hole, and after 69 days, the last miner (8) .................. . All 33 men were happy to (9) .................. .

 Student Book p.42

# 5 What's your style?

## Grammar reference

### Short comparative adjectives

| comparative adjective + *than* + noun |
|---|
| Sasha's hair is dark**er than** Kate's hair. |
| Kate's hair isn't long**er than** Sasha's hair. |
| Kate's pants are bagg**ier than** Sasha's jeans. |
| Sasha's shoes aren't low**er than** Kate's shoes. |

We use comparatives to talk about differences between two things or people.
Alex's hair is curlier than Toni's.
Short adjectives form short comparatives.
My cell phone is newer than Makiko's phone.

### Long comparative adjectives

| *more* + adjective + *than* |
|---|
| Luisa is **more competitive than** me. |
| Dieter is **more creative than** his sister. |

We use long comparatives to compare people and things with long adjectives.
Math is more difficult than history.
We form long comparatives with *more* + adjective + *than*.
Waterfalls are more beautiful than rivers.

### *(not) as … as*

| *(not) as* + adjective + *as* |
|---|
| I'm **as** tall **as** Tom. We're the same height. |
| Liu **isn't as** cheerful **as** Kelly. Kelly is more cheerful. |

We use (*not*) *as* … *as* to talk about similarities (or not) between people and things.
I'm as tall as Jay. We're both 1.60 m.
We form sentences with *(not) as* + adjective + *as*.
Swimming isn't as exciting as skiing.

## Word list

### Hair and clothes

baggy
curly
high
long
low
short
straight
tall
tight
wavy

### Personality adjectives

cheerful
competitive
creative
disorganized
helpful
sensitive
sociable
talkative

## Vocabulary

**1 Unscramble the words in the sentences.**

1 His hair is *long* ______ (glon) and ______ (ryulc).
2 She isn't ______ (hotrs). She's ______ (latl).
3 Her hair isn't ______ (tagirths). It's ______ (vywa).
4 His shirt isn't ______ (hitgt). It's ______ (gabgy).
5 Her boots aren't ______ (wol). They're ______ (gihh).

**2 Fill in the blanks with the words below.**

low short small ~~tall~~ tight wavy

Robert Pattinson is my favorite movie star. He's very (1) *tall* ______, about 1.85 m. He has (2) ______, blue eyes, and he has (3) ______, ______ dark hair. In the *Twilight* movies, he plays Edward Cullen. He wears (4) ______, black shoes, (5) ______ jeans, and a shirt.

**Extend your vocabulary**

**3 Label the clothes with the correct adjectives.**

flowery patterned plaid ~~plain~~ spotted striped

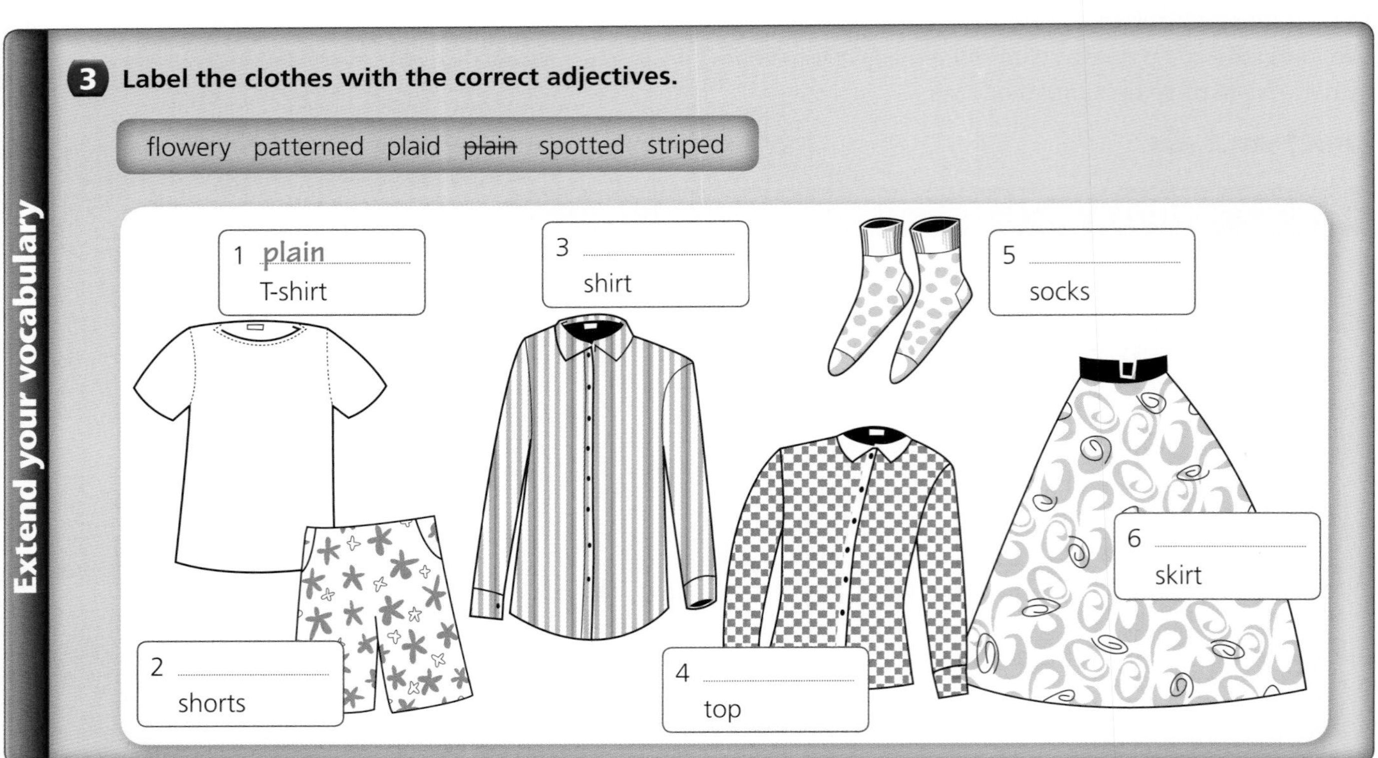

## Grammar

**1 Circle the correct comparative form of the adjectives.**

1 big → biger / bigger
2 short → shorter / shortier
3 curly → curlyer / curlier
4 good → gooder / better
5 hot → hotter / hoter
6 sad → sader / sadder

**2 Write the comparative form of the adjectives.**

1 funny → funnier
2 tight → ..........
3 fat → ..........
4 bad → ..........
5 baggy → ..........
6 easy → ..........

**3 Put the words in order to complete the sentences.**

1 bigger / is / London / than
New York is bigger than London.
2 tighter / my old jeans / than / are
My new jeans .......... .
3 is / Book 2 / than / easier
Book 1 .......... .
4 than / are / my classmates / noisier
My sister's classmates .......... .

**4 Look at the pictures and write sentences about Pamela and José. Use the words in parentheses.**

1 Pamela is shorter than José. (Pamela / short / José)
2 .......... . (José's jeans / tight / Pamela's jeans)
3 .......... . (Pamela's room / clean / José's room)
4 .......... . (José / thin / Pamela)
5 .......... . (Pamela's hair / long / José's hair)

# Vocabulary

## 1 Fill in the blanks with the personality adjectives below.

cheerful ~~competitive~~ creative disorganized helpful sensitive sociable talkative

1 He likes sports, but he doesn't like losing. He's competitive.
2 Her room is a mess, and her books and clothes are all over the floor. She's ________.
3 She's kind, and often does things for people. She's ________.
4 He loves playing the guitar and writing songs. He's ________.
5 Those children are never quiet. They're ________.
6 She knows when people aren't happy and tries to help them. She's ________.
7 He's always happy and he always smiles. He's very ________.
8 She loves going to parties. She's ________.

## 2 Circle the correct word.

1 Sandra loves being with people. She's very **sociable** / **disorganized**.
2 Suzy is more **sensitive** / **creative** than Maya. Suzy always understands my problems.
3 Kenji loves painting and making things. He's so **competitive** / **creative**.
4 I'm more **helpful** / **competitive** than my brother. I always want to win!
5 Julia uses her cell phone all the time. She's a **talkative** / **sensitive** person.
6 Are you as **disorganized** / **cheerful** as your sister? She's always smiling and happy.
7 I can't find anything in my room. I'm so **disorganized** / **talkative**.
8 My brother is very **helpful** / **creative**. He always sets the table.

**Extend your vocabulary**

## 3 Read the descriptions, and write the correct adjective.

~~bossy~~ hardworking lazy reliable shy stubborn

1 Lucia likes giving orders, and telling people what to do. bossy
2 Phil likes watching TV and playing computer games, but he doesn't like doing his homework! ________
3 Ray always studies a lot and does well in school. After school, he sometimes goes to the library to study! ________
4 Libby doesn't like vegetables. We just can't make her eat them. ________
5 Ruby doesn't like meeting new people. She has friends, but she doesn't like going to parties. ________
6 Rita always arrives to class on time. She always does her homework. If she says she's going to do something, she does it! ________

1

2

3

4

5

6

## Grammar

**1 Write the comparative form of the adjectives.**

1 helpful → *more helpful*
2 cold → ..........
3 sociable → ..........
4 difficult → ..........
5 thick → ..........
6 energetic → ..........
7 interesting → ..........
8 happy → ..........

**2 Look at the chart. Write comparative sentences about Ken, Sonja, and Tony. Use the words in parentheses.**

| Are you … | Ken | Sonja | Tony |
|---|---|---|---|
| competitive? | ✓✓✓ | ✓✓ | ✓ |
| sociable? | ✓ | ✓✓ | ✓✓✓ |
| lazy? | ✓ | ✓✓ | ✓✓ |
| helpful? | ✓✓ | ✓✓ | ✓✓✓ |
| reliable? | ✓✓ | ✓✓✓ | ✓ |
| creative? | ✓ | ✓✓✓ | ✓✓ |
| strong? | ✓✓✓ | ✓✓ | ✓ |

1 *Ken is more competitive than Tony*. (Ken / competitive / Tony)
2 ..........  . (Sonja / lazy / Ken)
3 ..........  . (Tony / sociable / Ken)
4 ..........  . (Sonja / reliable / Tony)
5 ..........  . (Sonja / creative / Ken)
6 ..........  . (Ken / strong / Sonja)

**3 Write sentences about Ken, Sonja, and Tony with *(not) as … as*.**

1 Ken / Sonja / creative
*Ken isn't as creative as Sonja*.

2 Sonja / strong / Tony
..........  .

3 Tony / competitive / Ken
..........  .

4 Sonja / sociable / Tony
..........  .

5 Ken / helpful / Sonja
..........  .

6 Sonja / lazy / Tony
..........  .

# Reading

**1** **Read the profiles. Match the profiles with the photos.**

## MY STYLE

A

B

C

1 I'm very creative, and I love wearing vintage clothes from the 1960s. I think vintage clothes are more stylish than modern clothes. I love the dresses and the different hair styles. I have long, straight hair, and I often wear my hair in a "beehive". Jennifer Lopez sometimes has her hair in this style, too! My favorite jacket has polka dots all over, and I usually wear it with a big belt. I love wearing high shoes, but sometimes it's difficult to walk in them! I can usually only wear these clothes to parties. ☹
**Karen, 16, Texas**

2 I have to wear a school uniform during the week. That's difficult for me because I'm a very cheerful person, and I like wearing colorful clothes. On the weekends, I love wearing patterned shirts and pants. My socks always reflect my personality during the week or on the weekend - they're always striped or spotted! ☺ **Leonardo, 16, Bahia**

3 I'm not as interested as other teenagers in clothes and fashion. I'm quite a disorganized and messy person. I think my clothes are a little messy, too! I like comfortable clothes. After school and on the weekends, I love wearing big baggy pants, and plain T-shirts. When I go to a party, I usually look better than this! ☺ **Joey, 16, Washington**

**2** **Circle the correct word.**

1 Karen likes **vintage** / **modern** clothes.
2 Karen has long, **wavy** / **straight** hair.
3 Joey likes **comfortable** / **fashionable** clothes.
4 Joey likes **baggy** / **patterned** pants.
5 Leonardo likes **colorful** / **plain** clothes.
6 Leonardo likes wearing **striped** / **flowery** socks.

**3** **Complete the sentences with the comparative form of the adjective in parentheses.**

1 Karen thinks modern clothes aren't *as* *stylish* *as* vintage clothes. (stylish)
2 Karen is ______ ______ ______ Joey. (creative)
3 Joey isn't ______ ______ ______ other teenagers in clothes. (interested)
4 Leonardo thinks colorful clothes are ______ ______ ______ plain clothes. (cheerful)

**4** **Who said it? Write K (Karen), J (Joey), or L (Leonardo).**

1 "I often wear my hair in the same style as Jennifer Lopez." *K*
2 "My clothes reflect my personality." ______
3 "I usually wear it with a big belt." ______
4 "I like comfortable clothes." ______
5 "My socks are always striped or spotted." ______
6 "My clothes are a little messy, too!" ______

# 6 Amazing places

## Grammar reference

### Superlative adjectives

| ***the* + superlative + noun** |
|---|
| It's **the largest** volcano on Earth. |
| It's **the most crowded** country in the world. |

We use superlative adjectives to talk about special things.
It is the best painting in the class.
The Pacific Ocean is the biggest ocean in the world.

### *should / shouldn't*

| **Affirmative** | **Negative** |
|---|---|
| You **should** use sunblock. | You **shouldn't** carry a lot of money. |
| **Questions** | **Answers** |
| **Should** I take a passport? | Yes, you **should**. / No, you **shouldn't**. |
| What clothes **should** I take? | You **should** take a jacket and boots. |

We use *should / shouldn't* to give advice.
You should see the doctor.
You shouldn't sit in the sun all day.
We use *should* with an infinitive.
You should go home.
The form of *should* is the same for all persons.
I should go home.
He should go home.
They should go home.
We use the question form *should* + *I / we* + verb to ask for advice.
Should I wear a jacket?
What should I wear?

## Word list

### Adjectives for places

crowded
deep
dry
large
modern
narrow
wet
wide

### Travel items

camera
e-ticket
guidebook
hiking boots
insect spray
passport
sunblock
swimsuit

# Vocabulary

**1 Find eight adjectives in the word snake.**

adwideonthcrowdedegenarrowstdeepridrywdblargeverwetbgamodernvty

**2 Fill in the blanks with adjectives in exercise 1.**

1 a wide river

2 a ________ building

3 a ________ window

4 a ________ dog

5 a ________ room

6 a ________ forest

7 a ________ hole

8 a ________ desert

## Extend your vocabulary

**3 Fill in the blanks with the words below.**

depth height ~~length~~ weight width

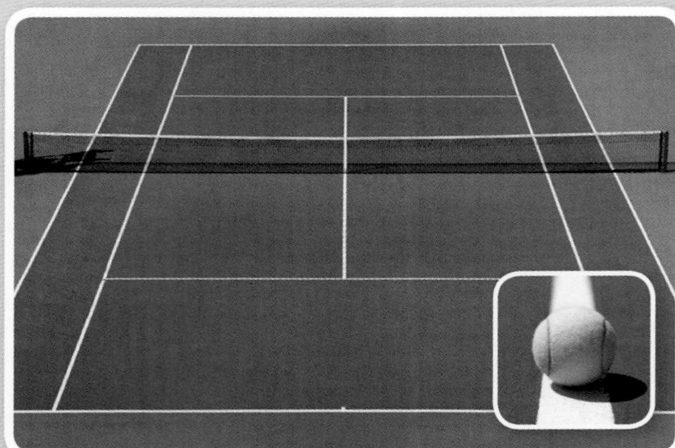

1 The length of a tennis court is about 23 meters.
2 The ________ of the net is about 1 meter.
3 The ________ of the ball is about 60 grams.

4 The length of an Olympic swimming pool is exactly 50 meters. The ________ is 25 meters.
5 The ________ of the water is at least two meters.

## Grammar

**1 Circle the correct words.**

1 That's the (deepest) / most deep swimming pool in the city.
2 She's the **helpfullest / most helpful** student in our class.
3 My brother is the **lazyest / laziest** person in our family.
4 This is **largest / the largest** house on the street.
5 *Bambi* is the **sadest / saddest** movie in the world!
6 This is the **cheapest / most cheap** DVD player in the store.

**2 Fill in the blanks with the superlative form of the adjectives below.**

bad expensive fat funny old ~~tall~~

1 He is the tallest student in our class.

2 *Comedy Hour* is ........................ show on TV!

3 Grandma is ........................ person in our family.

4 I'm ........................ player on our team!

5 That's ........................ camera in the store.

6 Rex is ........................ dog in our neighborhood!

**3 Fill in the blanks with the superlative form of the adjectives.**

1 Today is a hot day. It's the hottest day of the year.
2 That's a wide river. It's ........................ in the country.
3 Eiji is a talkative boy. He's ........................ in the class.
4 That's a big building. It's ........................ in the city.
5 Miss Jones is a young teacher. She's ........................ in the school.
6 Rikki's is a good restaurant. It's ........................ in town.

# Vocabulary

**1 Label the pictures with the words below.**

camera e-ticket guidebook ~~hiking boots~~ insect spray passport sunblock swimsuit

1 hiking boots

2 ..........

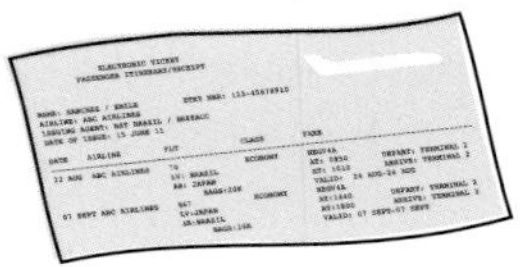

3 ..........

4 ..........

5 ..........

6 ..........

7 ..........

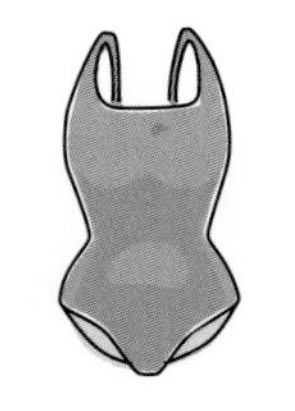

8 ..........

**2 Circle the correct words.**

1 I'm going to the mountains on the weekend. I'm going to take my **passport** / **hiking boots**.
2 You can't fly without **an e-ticket** / **a camera**.
3 Look at that amazing view! You should take a photo with your **camera** / **sunblock**.
4 Don't forget your **hiking boots** / **passport** when you travel abroad.
5 That river looks great, but I can't go swimming. I forgot my **guidebook** / **swimsuit**.
6 Everyone should wear **sunblock** / **insect spray** when it's sunny.

**Extend your vocabulary**

**3 Match the pictures with the words below.**

battery compass map raincoat sleeping bag ~~tent~~ flashlight

1  2  3  4  5  6  7

1 tent
2 ..........
3 ..........
4 ..........
5 ..........
6 ..........
7 ..........

# Grammar

**1** **Fill in the blanks with *should* or *shouldn't*.**

1 A: Ruth has a toothache. Should ________ she visit a doctor?
B: No, she ________. She ________ visit a dentist!

2 Timmy ________ go out in a T-shirt. It's cold and rainy. He ________ wear a raincoat!

3 Those students ________ walk in the street. It's dangerous! They ________ stay on the sidewalk.

4 A: Grandpa has a terrible cough. ________ he visit the doctor?
B: Yes, he ________.

**2** **Put the words in order to make sentences.**

1 should / early / You / go to bed
You should go to bed early.

2 a lot of coffee / People / drink / shouldn't
________.

3 Students / every evening / do their homework / should
________.

4 every day / shouldn't / You / eat fast food
________.

5 visit the dentist / Children / should / twice a year
________.

6 shouldn't / work / all the time / You
________.

**3** **Complete the online advice posts. Write questions and answers with *should* and the words in parentheses.**

1
I can't read magazines or newspapers. The writing is too small! What should I do ________?
(what / I / do) **Jeff, 65**
Maybe you need glasses. ________.
(you / visit / the eye doctor) **Cara, 67**

2
Richard is tired all the time. He doesn't have any energy. ________?
(what / he / do) **Richard's wife, 43**
________.
(he / exercise more) Running and swimming are good. **Stan, 45**

3
My friend and I want to visit Iceland.
________?
(when / we / go) **Mizuho, 23**
________.
(you / go / in the summer) Don't go in the winter – it's cold! **Jordi, 25**

4
Anna's new to this town. She wants to meet people. ________?
(where / she / go) **Marta, 16**
________.
(she / go / to the youth club). A lot of teenagers go there. **Stefano, 15**

## Reading

**1 Read the article quickly. Find the words and write the correct paragraphs.**

1 damage A
2 storms ______
3 dive ______
4 snorkel ______
5 sculptor ______
6 coral reef ______

# THE MOST UNUSUAL MUSEUM IN THE WORLD?

**A** Every year more than 750,000 visitors visit coral reefs in the Caribbean Sea, Mexico. They swim, and dive in the water. But these visitors are causing damage to the reef. People should do more to protect the coral reefs, but how?

**B** The answer is nine meters under the Pacific Ocean. It's the deepest and wettest museum in the world, and it is called the Cancun Underwater Museum. There's only one problem. You have to snorkel to visit it!

**C** On the bottom of the ocean, there are 400 statues of people. Local Mexican people were the models for the statues and all the statues are very heavy. When you dive down and visit the museum, you can swim between the statues, look at them from above, and sit next to them.

**D** A British sculptor made the statues from a special material. Coral grows on this material, so the statues are actually a new living coral reef! The statues attract new fish and sea creatures to come and live in this part of the ocean. Hurricanes and storms should not cause problems for the statues.

**E** So, what do you think? Is this the most unusual museum in the world?

**2 Circle the correct word.**

1 People **should** / **shouldn't** protect the coral reefs.
2 You **should** / **shouldn't** be able to snorkel to visit the museum.
3 People **should** / **shouldn't** visit the coral reef.
4 New fish **should** / **shouldn't** come to this part of the ocean.
5 Hurricanes and storms **should** / **shouldn't** damage the statues.

**3 Fill in the blanks with the superlative form of the adjectives below.**

deep heavy ~~interesting~~ unusual wet

1 "I love the idea! I think this is the most interesting museum in the world."
2 "It's under the ocean, so it's the ______ museum in the world."
3 "The museum is the ______ museum in the world – you have to snorkel to visit it!"
4 "Are the statues the ______ statues in the ocean?"
5 "Do you think this is the ______ museum in the world? I think it's strange"

**4 Are the sentences T (True) or F (False)? Correct the false sentences.**

1 The museum is in the Indian Ocean.
T / F The museum is in the Caribbean Sea.
2 There are 400 statues of people.
T / F ______
3 More than 750,000 people visit the Pacific Ocean every year.
T / F ______
4 You can't touch the statues.
T / F ______
5 Fish and other sea creatures don't like the statues.
T / F ______
6 An American sculptor made the statues.
T / F ______

 Student Book p.60

# 7 Sports world

## Grammar reference

### *be going to* (affirmative and negative)

| Affirmative | Negative |
|---|---|
| I'**m going to** play volleyball. | I'**m not going to** play volleyball. |
| You'**re going to** do gymnastics. | You **aren't going to** do gymnastics. |
| He'**s going to** go swimming. | She **isn't going to** go swimming. |
| We'**re going to** play tennis. | They **aren't going to** play tennis. |
| You'**re going to** do track and field. | You **aren't going to** do track and field. |
| They'**re going to** go running. | They **aren't going to** go running. |

We use *be going to* to talk about plans and resolutions.
I'm going to pass the test.
She's going to do more exercise.
We form *be going to* sentences with subject + *be* + *going to* + infinitive.
Matt is going to learn to snowboard.
They aren't going to go to the pool later.

### *be going to* (questions)

| Questions | Answers |
|---|---|
| **Am** I **going to** do exercise every day? | Yes, I **am**. / No, I'**m not**. |
| **Is** he **going to** practice today? | Yes, he **is**. / No, he **isn't**. |
| **Are** we **going to** wear pads? | Yes, we **are**. / No, we **aren't**. |
| What **is** she **going to** do? | She'**s going to** play tennis. |
| When **are** they **going to** play? | They'**re going to** play today. |

We use *yes / no* questions to ask about plans and resolutions.
Are you going to play soccer on the weekend?
We form *yes / no* questions with *be* + subject + *going to* + infinitive.
Is she going to leave the team?

## Word list

### Sports

basketball
cycling
field hockey
gymnastics
snowboarding
track and field
volleyball
waterskiing

### Sports equipment

gloves
goggles
helmet
lifejacket
pads
sneakers
tracksuit
wetsuit

## Vocabulary

**1 Find eight sports in the word snake.**

trackandfieldbasketballsnowboardingfieldhockeyvolleyballcyclinggymnasticswaterskiing

**2 Write the correct sports for each description.**

1 You do this sport when it's cold. snowboarding
2 You do this sport on a lake or on the ocean. ..............................
3 You can dance, jump, and balance in this sport. ..............................
4 This sport includes the high jump, the long jump, and the 100 meter race. ..............................
5 You can play this on the beach, or in the gym. ..............................
6 You do this sport on two wheels. ..............................

Extend your vocabulary

**3 Fill in the blanks with the verbs below.**

bounce catch ~~drop~~ miss save throw

1 Don't drop the ball!

2 Don't .............................. the goal!

3 In baseball, you have to .............................. the ball.

4 The goalkeeper has to .............................. goals.

5 In bowling, you have to .............................. the ball.

6 In basketball, you can .............................. the ball.

# Grammar

| | Jess | Chuck | Kylie and Ricky |
|---|---|---|---|
| **Monday** | | go swimming | go swimming |
| **Tuesday** | play tennis | play soccer | visit Aunt Jill |
| **Wednesday** | do karate | watch a baseball game | drive to the shopping mall |
| **Thursday** | go climbing | go swimming | watch movies |
| **Friday** | take photos | buy a new skateboard | have dinner at a restaurant |
| **Saturday** | have a party | have a party | play golf |
| **Sunday** | | go on vacation! | |



**1 Look at the chart. Who says these sentences?**

1 "I'm going to buy a new skateboard on Friday." Chuck

2 "We aren't going to play golf on Saturday. We're going to have a party!" ______ and ______

3 "I'm going to do karate on Wednesday." ______

4 "I'm not going to go climbing on Thursday. I'm going to go swimming on Thursday." ______

5 "We're going to play golf on Saturday." ______ and ______

6 "We're going to go swimming on Monday." ______, ______, and ______

**2 Circle the correct words.**

1 Kylie and Ricky **are** / **aren't** going to have a party on Saturday.
2 Chuck **isn't** / **aren't** going to play tennis on Tuesday.
3 Kylie and Ricky **is** / **are** going to watch movies on Thursday.
4 Jess and Chuck **isn't** / **aren't** going to sunbathe on Monday.
5 Jess **is** / **are** going to take photos on Friday.
6 Kylie and Ricky **are** / **aren't** going to go on vacation on Sunday.

**3 Put the words in order to make sentences.**

1 sister / going / My / tomorrow / go / to / is / waterskiing
My sister is going to go waterskiing tomorrow.

2 karate class / to / tonight / to / not / I'm / go / going
______.

3 friends / weekend / the / They're / meet / to / on / their / going
______.

4 to / afternoon / play / Sam's / this / going / basketball
______.

5 going / summer / on / We / vacation / year / to go / aren't / this
______.

6 Wednesday / soccer / You / on / aren't / to / going / play
______.

# Vocabulary

**1 Label the pictures with the words below.**

gloves goggles helmet ~~lifejacket~~ pads sneakers tracksuit wetsuit

1 lifejacket

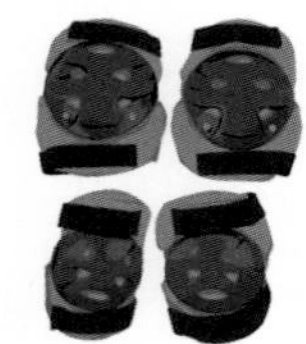

2 ..................

3 ..................

4 ..................

5 ..................

6 ..................

7 ..................

8 ..................

**2 Fill in the blanks with the correct words from exercise 1.**

1 A: I'm going waterskiing on the weekend.
B: Wear a lifejacket !

2 A: Let's go cycling after school!
B: Good idea! Can I borrow a .................., please?

3 A: I hate swimming. The water hurts my eyes.
B: Why don't you wear ..................?

4 A: Why are you wearing your ..................?
B: I'm going to go running.

5 A: I went snowboarding last winter.
B: Did you have to wear .................. to protect your hands?

6 A: I'm going to swim across the lake for charity.
B: Wear a ................... The water is very cold!

## Extend your vocabulary

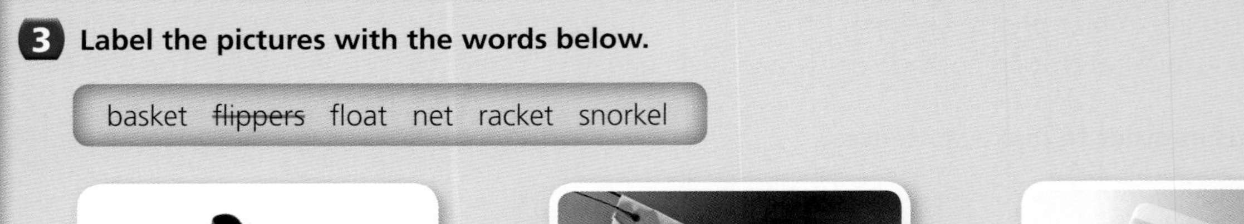

**3 Label the pictures with the words below.**

basket ~~flippers~~ float net racket snorkel

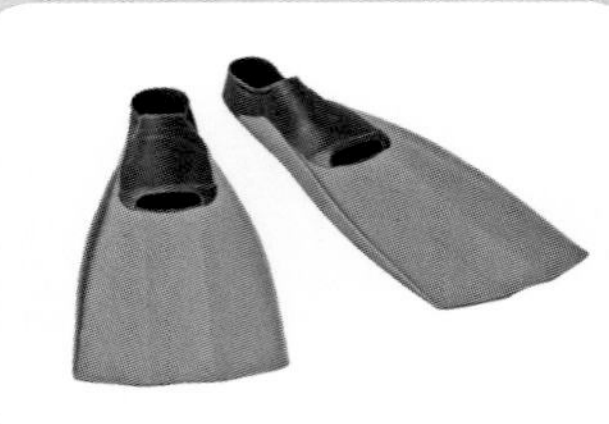

1 flippers

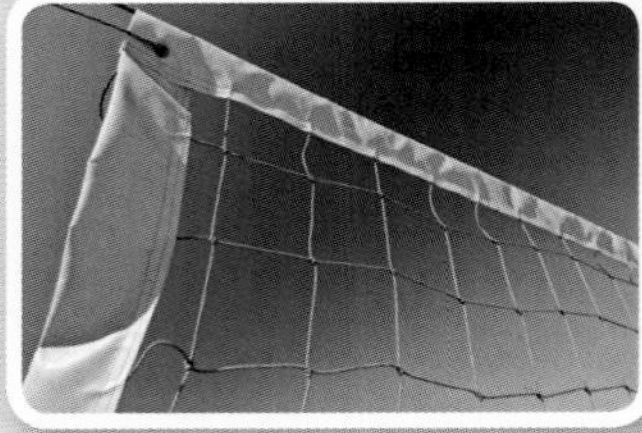

2 ..................

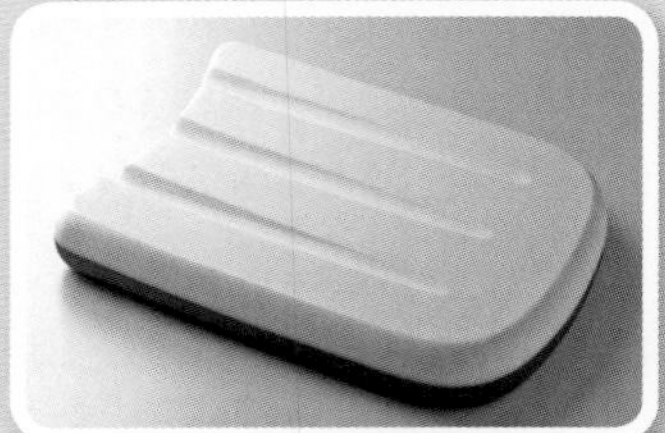

3 ..................

4 ..................

5 ..................

6 ..................

# Grammar

**1 Write questions with *be going to* and the words in parentheses.**

1 What is Suki going to do ............ on Tuesday? (What / Suki / do)
She's going to play tennis.

2 ............ on Monday? (What / Jake and Brad / do)
They're going to go cycling.

3 ............ on Saturday at the mall? (What / Lee / buy)
He's going to buy a new cell phone.

4 ............ (When / they / visit their grandparents)
They're going to visit their grandparents on Sunday.

5 ............ on Wednesday night? (Jana / do karate)
Yes, she is.

6 ............ after class? (Lidia and Steve / play soccer)
No, they aren't.

**2 Look at the chart. Complete the questions. Then write the short answers about the sports camp.**

| | Rob | Luis | Olivia |
|---|---|---|---|
| **Saturday morning** | | | |
| **Saturday afternoon** | | | |
| **Sunday morning** | | | |
| **Sunday afternoon** | | | |

1 Are ...... we going ...... to go cycling on Saturday morning? Yes, we are ...... .
2 ...... we ...... to visit a museum on Saturday afternoon? ...... .
3 ...... Luis ...... play field hockey on Saturday afternoon? ...... .
4 ...... Olivia ...... play soccer on Sunday morning? ...... .
5 ...... Rob and Luis ...... go cycling on Sunday morning? ...... .
6 ...... they ...... go swimming on Sunday afternoon? ...... .

**3 Complete the conversation.**

Rita: I'm going to go to the mountains next weekend.
Arturo: (1) Are you going to go climbing?
Rita: Yes, I (2) ...... . But my brother isn't. He (3) ...... swimming.
Arturo: (4) ...... stay in a hotel?
Rita: No, (5) ...... . Don't be silly! We (6) ...... stay in a tent.
Arturo: When (7) ...... come home?
Rita: We (8) ...... come home on Sunday night.
Arturo: Have a great time!

# Reading

**1 Read the texts quickly. Match the pictures with the texts.**

1 ........ 2 ........ 3 ........

**A** Last year I played field hockey for my school team, but this year I'm going to learn to play underwater hockey! I have to wear a snorkel, flippers, and special gloves. You play underwater hockey in a swimming pool, and we're going to start training next week. It's just like field hockey, but it's all underwater! It isn't easy, and I'm going to have to learn to hit the ball (called a "puck") under the water, and breathe with my snorkel, too! **Daisuke, Tokyo**

**C** We're going to play sepak takraw next week for the first time. It's gymnastics, soccer, and volleyball all in one game! You need a special takraw ball, and you have to hit the ball over a net with your legs, back, head, or feet. It's going to be hard work playing this game, but a lot of fun! **Hao-yu and Chen, Seoul**

**B** This summer I'm going to learn joggling with two of my friends. Joggling is a mixture of jogging and juggling. It looks easy, but it's really difficult. You have to jog, and throw balls in the air at the same time. If you drop a ball you have to stop, pick it up, and start again. One day, I'm going to enter the Joggling World Championships.
**Roberto, Veracruz**

**2 Circle the correct answers.**

1 Daisuke is going to learn to play **field** / **underwater** hockey.
2 Daisuke is going to wear a **snorkel** / **helmet**.
3 Roberto is going to learn to joggle with **his friends** / **his family**.
4 Hao-yu is going to play **soccer** / **sepak takraw** next week.

**3 Answer the questions with short answers.**

1 Is Daisuke going to learn to play field hockey this year? No, he isn't.
2 Is he going to play underwater hockey? ..................
3 Is Roberto going to learn to jog? ..................
4 Is Roberto going to enter a championship this year? ..................
5 Are Hao-yu and Chen going to a gymnastics club next week? ..................
6 Are Hao-yu and Chen going to have fun? ..................

**4 Find the mistakes. Then correct the sentences.**

1 You play underwater hockey in a ~~lake~~. You play underwater hockey in a swimming pool.
2 You have to wear a snorkel, flippers, and wetsuit for underwater hockey. ..................
3 If you drop the ball in joggling, you can continue. ..................
4 Joggling is like jogging and gymnastics. ..................
5 You can use a soccer ball to play sepak takraw. ..................
6 You play sepak takraw with your legs only. ..................

 Student Book p.70

# 8 Having fun

## Grammar reference

### Present progressive for the future

| Affirmative | Negative |
|---|---|
| I'**m meeting** Paulo on Friday. | I'**m not meeting** Sam on Friday. |
| He'**s going** to a concert later. | He **isn't going** to a party later. |
| **Questions** | **Answers** |
| **Are** you **going** to the theater tonight? | Yes, I **am**. / No, I'**m not**. |
| What time **are** you **taking** the bus? | I'**m taking** the bus at six o'clock. |

We use time expressions with the present progressive to talk about future arrangements.
They're going to the music festival tonight.
She's meeting Mary-Anne for a picnic later.

### *I'd like … / Would you like …?*

| Affirmative + infinitive | Questions and answers |
|---|---|
| I'**d like to go** to the movies. | **Would** you **like to go** to the movies? |
| We'**d like to see** a comedy. | **Would** you **like to see** a comedy? |
| | Yes, please. / No, thanks. |

| Affirmative + noun | Questions and answers |
|---|---|
| I'**d like** a hamburger. | **Would** you **like** a hamburger? |
| They'**d like** two drinks. | **Would** they **like** two drinks? |
| She'**d like** some chocolate. | **Would** she **like** some chocolate? |
| | Yes, please. / No, thanks. |

We use …*'d like* to make requests. It is a polite way to say *I want*.
I'd like to see a scary movie.
I'd like some popcorn.
We use *Would you like …?* to make offers.
Would you like some chocolate?
We use *some* before uncountable nouns for offers.
Would you like some soda?

## Word list

### Fun events

art exhibition
baseball game
birthday party
fashion show
music festival
parade
picnic
stage play

### Kinds of movies

action movie
animated movie
comedy
fantasy movie
horror movie
musical
mystery
science fiction movie

8

# Vocabulary

**1 Match 1–6 with a–f to make fun events.**

1 baseball — d
2 music
3 fashion
4 birthday
5 art
6 stage

a party
b play
c exhibition
d game
e show
f festival

**2 What are they planning to do on the weekend? Correct the sentences with words from exercise 1.**

1 We're going to a ~~fashion show~~! *baseball game*

2 They're going to an art exhibition. ______

3 She's having a picnic. ______

4 You're going to a music festival. ______

5 We're going to see a parade. ______

6 I'm going to a fashion show. ______

## Extend your vocabulary

**3 Label the pictures with the verbs below.**

blow out candles   blow up balloons   decorate a room   ~~give presents~~   make a home movie   wrap presents

1 *give presents*

2 ______

3 ______

4 ______

5 ______

6 ______

## Grammar

**1** **Look at Kelly's and Bill's plans for tomorrow. Complete the questions with the present progressive form. Then write short answers.**

1 Is ______ Kelly having ______ a guitar lesson at 4 p.m. tomorrow? No, she isn't ______.
2 ______ Bill ______ soccer tomorrow morning? ______.
3 ______ Bill and Chris ______ dinner at 7 p.m.? ______.
4 ______ Kelly ______ tennis at 10 a.m.? ______.
5 ______ Kelly and Brad ______ a rock concert in the evening? ______.
6 ______ Bill ______ to the dentist at 3 p.m.? ______.

**2** **Correct the sentences about Kelly and Bill's plans for tomorrow. Use the present progressive affirmative and negative forms.**

1 Kelly is having a picnic with Martha.
She isn't having a picnic with Martha. She's having a picnic with Katy.
2 Bill is meeting Marina in the library.
He ______. He ______ at the cybercafé.
3 Kelly and Brad are going to a music festival in the morning.
They ______.
______.
4 Kelly is going to the dentist at 10:30 a.m.
______.
______.
5 Bill and Anya are having dinner at 8:30 p.m.
______.
______.

**3** **Bill and Kelly are chatting online. Complete their chat with the present progressive form of the verbs in parentheses.**

**Bill:** Hi, Kelly. (1) Are ______ you playing ______ (play) tennis tomorrow?
**Kelly:** Hi, Bill. Yes, I am. But I (2) ______ (go) the dentist first.
**Bill:** Really? What time (3) ______ you ______ (go) the dentist?
**Kelly:** At 9:30 a.m. What about you? What (4) ______ you ______ (do) tomorrow?
**Bill:** I (5) ______ (play) soccer in the morning. Then I (6) ______ (go) to the movies.
**Kelly:** (7) ______ Anya ______ (go) with you?
**Bill:** Yes, she is. Would you like to come, too?
**Kelly:** I'd love to, but I can't. I (8) ______ (meet) Brad in the evening. We (9) ______ (go) to a music festival!

# Vocabulary

**1 Unscramble the letters and find the kinds of movies.**

1 usaclim m u s i c a l
2 tcnioa vomei ______ ______
3 yestrym ______
4 santafy ivmeo ______ ______
5 domecy ______
6 maniadet evimo ______ ______

**2 What kinds of movies are they talking about?**

1 "I loved the little blue cat. He was so cute." animated movie
2 "I love all the songs and the dancing." ______
3 "Who did the crime? The detectives have to find the answer." ______
4 "We didn't stop laughing all night." ______
5 "My sister was really scared. She wanted to leave before the end." ______
6 "The special effects were amazing. I loved the robots." ______

Extend your vocabulary

**3 Match the pictures with the words below.**

camera operator graphic designer ~~make-up artist~~
movie director sound engineer storyboard artist

1 make-up artist
2 ______
3 ______
4 ______
5 ______
6 ______


Student Book p.76

## Grammar

**1 What would they like? Follow the lines and complete the sentences. Then write the names.**

1 He'd like ........ some juice. Juan ........
2 ........ some ice cream. ........
3 ........ a bottle of water. ........
4 ........ a banana. ........
5 ........ some pizza. ........
6 ........ an apple. ........

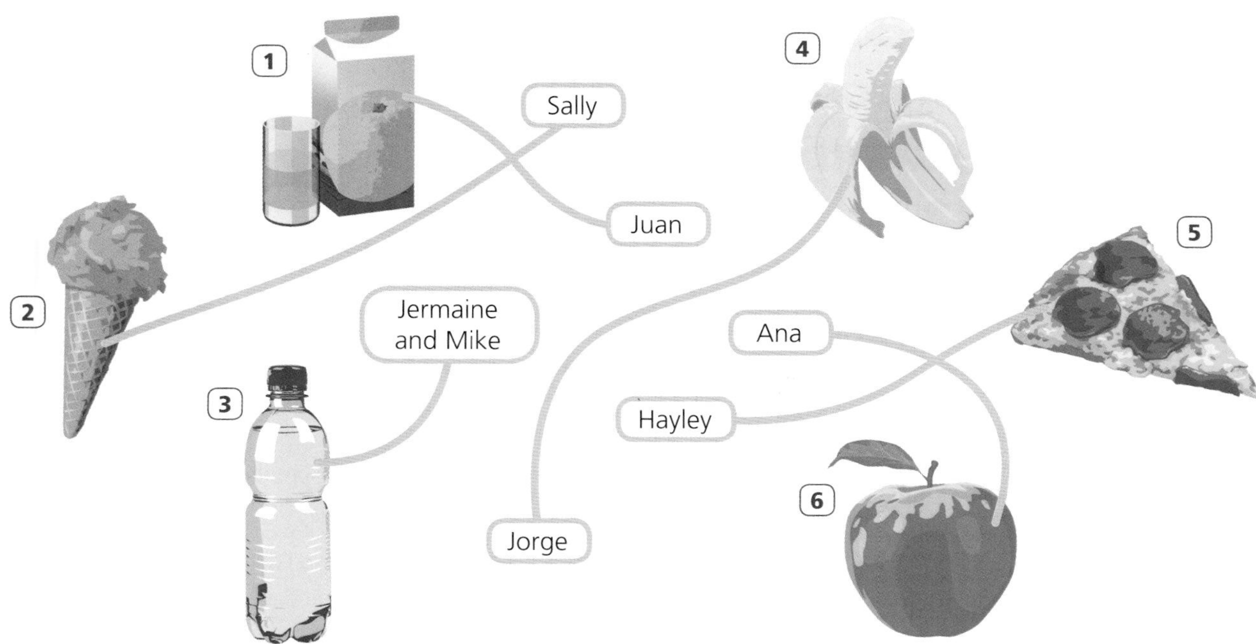


**2 Write offers and complete the replies.**

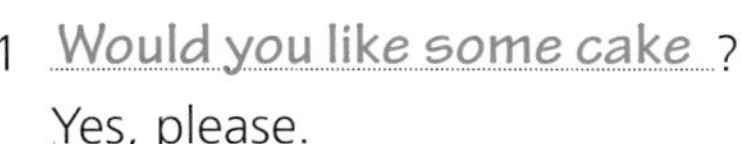

1 Would you like some cake ? Yes, please.

2 ........ ........? No, ........ .

3 ........ ........? Yes, ........ .

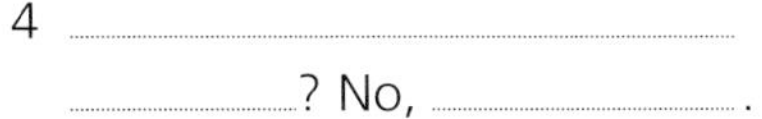

4 ........ ........? No, ........ .

5 ........ ........? Yes, ........ .

6 ........ ........? No, ........ .

**3 Write the requests. Then answer them.**

1 pizza for lunch (✓) Would you like some pizza for lunch ? Yes, please .
2 a new cell phone (✓) ........ ? ........ .
3 some more homework (✗) ........ ? ........ .
4 a pet dog (✗) ........ ? ........ .
5 to go to a movie (✓) ........ ? ........ .
6 borrow my magazine (✗) ........ ? ........ .

## Reading

**1 Read the comments quickly. Match the people with the movies.**

1 Karina — d
2 Jed
3 Jackson
4 Sofia

a *Ocean Adventure*
b *The Coach*
c *The Missing Necklace*
d *North Pole 2*

# Which movies would they like to see on the weekend?

I'd like to see an animated movie, but I'd also like to see a movie with some action! I don't want to see a horror movie. I hate horror movies. They're too scary for me! An animated movie with good voices, and a little bit of action – perfect! **Karina, Boston**

I'm going to my friend's house for a movie party on the weekend. I'd like to watch an action movie. I love action movies. I saw *Pirates of the Caribbean 3* in the movie theater four times. I have a DVD of another new movie about pirates. We should watch it this weekend!
**Jed, San Antonio**

I'm going to the movie theater with my friend, Alex, on Saturday. He wants to see a science fiction movie. I really don't like science fiction movies. There's a good mystery movie I'd like to see. I love mystery movies. I like trying to figure out the answers. I hope Alex likes mysteries, too!
**Jackson, Calgary**

I don't like action movies, so I'd like to see a funny movie on the weekend. I love comedies, and I love animals. I don't mind if it isn't an animated comedy, but I'd really like to see a funny movie. **Sofia, Belo Horizonte**

**2 Read again. Write the correct responses.**

1 "Jed, would you like to see an action movie this weekend?" Yes, please.
2 "Karina, would you like to see a horror movie?" ______.
3 "Jackson, would you like to see a science fiction movie later?" ______.
4 "Sofia, would you like to see a comedy tonight?" ______.

**3 Circle the correct words.**

1 Karina doesn't like **action** / **horror** movies.
2 Jed likes **fantasy** / **action** movies.
3 Jackson doesn't like **science fiction** / **mystery** movies.
4 Sofia likes **action movies** / **comedies**.
5 Karina likes **action** / **fantasy** movies.
6 Sofia would like to see a **comedy** / **mystery**.

**4 Correct the sentences.**

1 Karina would like to see a horror movie. Karina wouldn't like to see a horror movie.
2 Jed is going to a birthday party at his friend's house. ______
3 Jackson loves horror movies. ______
4 Sofia loves robots. ______
5 The voices in animated movies aren't important for Karina. ______
6 Jed saw *Pirates of the Caribbean 3* five times. ______

 Student Book p.78